LEADERSHIP
ANATOMY
—— *in* ——
MOTION

Empowering
You to Lead
Through
Technology
and People

LEADERSHIP
ANATOMY
—— *in* ——
MOTION

LOUISA LORAN

FC

**FAST
COMPANY**
Press

Published by Fast Company Press
New York, New York
www.fastcompanypress.com

Distributed by Greenleaf Book Group

For ordering information or special discounts for bulk purchases, please contact Greenleaf Book Group at PO Box 91869, Austin, TX 78709, 512.891.6100.

Design and composition by Greenleaf Book Group and Chase Quarterman
Cover design by Greenleaf Book Group and Chase Quarterman
Author photo by Tue Schioerring
Part-opening illustrations by Oliva Bendtsen Cano

Publisher's Cataloging-in-Publication data is available.

Hardcover ISBN: 978-1-63908-151-6

Paperback ISBN: 978-1-63908-152-3

eBook ISBN: 978-1-63908-153-0

To offset the number of trees consumed in the printing of our books, Greenleaf donates a portion of the proceeds from each printing to the Arbor Day Foundation. Greenleaf Book Group has replaced over 50,000 trees since 2007.

Printed in the United States of America on acid-free paper

25 26 27 28 29 30 31 32   10 9 8 7 6 5 4 3 2 1

First Edition

To Morgan and Elliot,
my eternal motivation to make the reality amazing

CONTENTS

INTRODUCTION

The world is measured by winners and losers. Every day there is a quest to sell more, claim more, and save more money. Quick fixes are pitched in boardrooms all over the world, yet despite all the discussion and effort, the results rarely reflect the same enthusiasm. Leaders make decisions with the best intentions, yet too often without the necessary context or clarity.

Meanwhile, as the world moves forward with pace, businesses are either evolving or stagnating. Geopolitical watchpoints are omnipresent, financial markets navigate uncertainty, global trade is shifting, and competitive forces are being challenged on ideals more than ever before. A few years ago, the world seemed consumed by the pandemic—now, it is already a historical reference. Artificial intelligence (AI) is emerging as the defining technological theme of this era. And while everyone agrees it will be transformational, no one knows exactly how much, where, or when.

Instead of debating the scale of change or whether this is an exciting or challenging time, let's just say it is clear that many forces are in motion. In response, some business and leadership strategies cling to familiar models, while others experiment—not all with clear intent.

In today's business landscape, there is an undeniable bias toward activity. We are conditioned to believe that the more we do, the more valuable we are. Yet this relentless focus on busyness often leads to a disconnect between effort and meaningful results. Too often, I have experienced people working hard and organizations that are caught up in an endless cycle of movement—strategies are debated, projects are launched, and tactics are deployed—but without a clear understanding of the wider movements, lasting value often remains out of reach.

The principle of busyness can be deceptive. A good executive operates like a duck—calm on the surface while moving quickly below the waterline. Yet I rarely see this uniform pacesetting at all levels of an organization. Instead, the illusion of productivity creates a fog of inefficiency, hiding wasted efforts and missed opportunities. As leaders, do we ask ourselves often enough whether we are "just" busy or whether we are effectively setting ourselves up to win?

Every leader is trying. Yet, too often, different layers of the business have conflicting answers about what truly matters. When priorities are unclear and misaligned, decisions become misguided, and activity takes precedence over impact. The pressure to show momentum often drives a flow of initiatives, a flurry of fragmented efforts, cycles of "transformation projects," and repeated capability mappings—often carried out by different consultants. Despite the best intentions, both from those initiating the work and from those delivering it, many initiatives become exercises in activity rather than vehicles for meaningful progress, driven by a desire to catch up with market shifts and rising expectations, both of ourselves and of those around us.

I have had the privilege of working in leadership roles across sectors, industries, and geographies, including at organizations such as Google, Maersk, and Diageo. Through these experiences and working closely with customers, I have seen a broad range of approaches and patterns in successful change. Across these roles, I've contributed to shifts that grew revenue, repositioned legacy businesses, and helped accelerate technology adoption—often in environments where performance outpaced the broader industry. Having worked inside a luxury goods company, a leading consumer goods company, an industrial operational mastodon, and a scale-up tech company turned huge, I have also witnessed firsthand just how differently opportunities can be perceived, depending on the context of those doing the perceiving. This can lead to efforts that—despite their ambition—will never achieve the desired impact, instead leading to either missed opportunities or underestimated risks.

Some may call it boldness, others experience, but I've found that over time, even a single conversation with a well-informed team can reveal whether a strategic transformation will succeed or fail. Patterns emerge, and the same challenges tend to surface across industries and organizations. I share some of these in this book, not to prescribe solutions, but to equip leaders with reflections to help them navigate complexity and increase their likelihood of achieving meaningful progress.

When it comes to navigating business change, four distinct behaviors stand out to me: *envisioning* the future, *expanding* into possibilities, *steering* decisively, and *embodying* the change. Many business leaders excel in one but not the others and neglect opportunities from this narrower lens. When overplayed, each of these four behaviors carries an equal risk of becoming a limitation, creating business without impact. However, when these four behaviors are balanced, they become a true force multiplier. In fact, companies with a broad skill base significantly outperform their peers in profitability and impact.

CHASING EVERY IDEA, CATCHING NONE

Opportunities are everywhere in a fast-moving market, and when *visioning* goes wrong, the temptation to chase all your options is real. I have seen many leaders with a bias toward action and a focus on the sheer pace of change. Their businesses are constantly launching new initiatives, each backed by a compelling boardroom presentation. There is often a natural pull from leaders and top talent toward the latest opportunity—to have their names tied to the latest transformation, the newest strategy, the boldest pivot. Yet, too often, these efforts, without adequate complementarity, pile up without truly lifting the trajectory of the business.

A 2018 MIT Sloan study reports that only 28 percent of managers can name their company's top priorities.[1] Too often, the very tools designed to drive success often create noise instead. Leadership isn't just about setting things in motion—it is about making sure what's set in motion actually represents the best opportunities possible.

There is a fundamental difference between the organizations that can harness change and the ones that are overwhelmed by it. The first group is curious to find ideas but doesn't chase them all. Instead, they filter, focus, and execute. The second either hides and hopes for the storm to pass or confuses motion with momentum, taking comfort in growing lists of initiatives instead of real adaptability. And in a fast-moving market, being busy with everything is often worse than doing nothing at all.

The AI boom is another accelerator of this kind of blinded behavior. When everything sounds possible, no one wants to risk missing the train. So lists grow—hundreds of ideas, endless use cases, consultants brought in to explore them—only for the cycle to continue with more meetings, more discussions on what to prioritize, and ultimately, the realization that there aren't enough people to execute it all. Good intentions, poorly directed efforts. All while simpler, proven models such as document search and conversational AI could have already been implemented using a company's own data, allowing the organization to learn and adapt together.

IS IGNORANCE BLISS?

Lack of *expansive* thinking is another common driver of effort without impact that I encounter a lot. When businesses, teams, or leaders operate in isolation—measuring success by their own internal metrics rather than reality—it is easy to fall into the trap of believing that, as long as the numbers look good on paper, progress is being made. But growth that happens in a vacuum rarely lasts. Whether applied to strategy, product development, or commercial execution, the real measure of success isn't how well a company operates on its own terms—it is how well it aligns with the needs and expectations of the world around it.

I saw the truth of this firsthand in an industry-leading company with more than a century of winning experience. Profitability was under pressure—not just for them but across the industry. A relentless focus on efficiency meant customers were switching between competitors based on the best offer at the time. Churn was eating into margins. The data was there. I was CMO and VP of business development, and one of my teams, Customer Insights, had everything needed to show what was driving customer behavior. But, as always, having the "right answer" wasn't enough. It was still just the customer's voice, while the rest of the business was busy optimizing for cost.

This gap became impossible to ignore during a session with the global commercial leaders. The commercial leadership team meeting began by splitting the leaders into two groups—one representing the company, the other representing customers—and then they were asked to map expectations onto a Venn diagram, with one circle for what customers valued and were willing to pay for and the other for what the company wanted to offer. It was understood that there were disconnects, but no one predicted the degree of the gap. A shocking revelation arose. Together, we repeated the exercise for four different customer groups. The center of three out of the four Venn diagrams remained completely empty. It seemed that what the company offered and what customers valued did not intersect.

This wasn't just a misalignment—it was a fundamental problem. Customer-facing teams were bending over backward to close deals, trying to compensate for a value proposition that didn't resonate. The assumption had been that the business's market presence alone would secure long-term success. The reality? The company did not control the levers to remain competitive while protecting the margin, and the positioning was not sustainable. This wake-up call led to a complete shift in focus. Over the next five years, its Net Promoter Score (NPS) moved from −20 percent to +23 percent, and along with favorable market shifts, profits quadrupled. People were still busy, but now with a clear direction and a path to value.

I've seen the same pattern across industries. Every department can justify its work, but how often do teams stop and flip the lens? While leading strategic business transformation for Google, we partnered with a globally renowned retailer. During our work with them, we discovered that one team was focusing on increasing customer basket size by making adjacent products more competitive. Meanwhile, another team—measured on reducing order changes—was penalizing customers for adjusting their orders. The result? When customers responded positively to the first team's efforts, they were hit with extra fees from the second. Orders were canceled, and all the effort from both teams was wasted. Everyone was busy, but the business lost.

It happens everywhere—customer service and finance, product and marketing, sales and supply chain. There are promotions for products that never get developed, services that end up frustrating customers because of how they're billed, and teams working hard at canceling each other out. The issue isn't a lack of effort. We can call it a lack of *alignment*, but I believe it is mainly a lack of being open to seeing things from a wider perspective. Narrow views create blind spots.

Being busy in a silo might make for an impressive presentation, but it doesn't build a sustainable business. Progress requires a willingness to challenge assumptions, to see the bigger picture, and to create alignment across efforts. Businesses that do this well don't just grow—they build something that is positioned to evolve with the market. The risk of staying insular goes beyond inefficiency: Missed partnerships can mean falling behind while you watch competitors leverage collaboration to accelerate their innovation and scale faster.

MANAGEMENT FOR MANAGEMENT'S SAKE

When *steering* is misunderstood, the quest to improve efficiency and accountability can become an end in itself. The assumption is that if something is measured, reported on, and optimized, it must be improving. If dashboards look green and meetings are booked, progress must be happening. But when management turns into a machine that sustains itself, rather than enabling the business, it creates more drag than lift. Control does not automatically lead to business. And reporting is not enough reason to justify a whole layer in an organization. But too often, I have seen management become its own justification to exist, anchored in past decisions and focused on keeping existing wheels turning rather than understanding what is really needed.

Why does this happen? The pressure to "do something" is a powerful force. Leaders want to demonstrate control, teams want to show progress, and before long, the process itself takes priority over the outcome. Key performance indicators (KPIs)—or, at a higher level, objectives and key results (OKRs)—are intended as tools for focus, but they often turn into a balancing act between ambition and what can be measured or a truth that is clung to when real momentum is not felt. The irony is that all this management activity can create the illusion of control when, in reality, it often distracts from the real signs management needs to see and actions it must take. The business may feel like it is steering forward, but in practice, it is reacting to itself. The result is rarely either enhancement of the business's market position or improvement of individual skills.

The problem isn't measurement; it's mistaking measurement for progress. The most successful businesses aren't the ones with the most data, but the ones that know how to use that data to make better decisions. Data alone doesn't drive change—people do. When managing becomes more about justifying the past than shaping the future, organizations risk draining the energy from those who actually hold the potential to drive real change.

Acclaimed business advisor, Roger Martin, in his analysis of top CEOs, pointed to a defining trait: They are not widely busy.[2] Not because they have less responsibility, but because they focus on what truly drives impact. No seasoned leader would argue with that, yet the management structures further

The problem isn't measurement; it's mistaking measurement for progress.

down in organizations rarely role model this. A lack of timely steering often creates an unspoken delay in difficult decisions, allowing hesitation and bureaucracy to creep in. As a result, teams retreat and cling onto familiar structures—not out of conviction, but as a reflex against uncertainty. This reluctance to act is not always intentional. Laziness in business is not just about doing nothing—it is about defaulting to compliance over progress, mistaking oversight for leadership, and allowing potential to drain away under the weight of unnecessary complexity. Breaking a problem into ever-smaller pieces doesn't necessarily make it more manageable. More often, it just makes the problem more fragmented and harder to resolve.

In fast-changing environments where uncertainty is high and psychological safety is no longer a given, I have seen leadership shift from driving progress to simply keeping things afloat. When the organization's priorities keep shifting and no one feels confident enough to take a stand, momentum stalls. This outcome is not what leadership has hoped for. The business does keep moving, but it does so without a strong rhythm or direction. As a result, no one can tell whether this is a tweak, a turn, or a break. Over time, this condition is not merely inefficient, it becomes a state of adaptation rather than ambition. Energy disperses. The organization responds to change but doesn't shape it.

THE VOID OF LEADERSHIP

When we as leaders fail to *embody* change, we may make decisions, and our businesses may keep running, yet nothing truly takes root. When leadership lacks conviction, the organization learns to wait rather than act. Decisions are deferred, ownership is diluted, and instead of building toward a future, businesses settle into cycles of maintenance or survival. The result isn't outright failure, but it is a slow decline, where the organization's relevance fades before leadership even recognizes the urgency. Often, by the time alarm bells ring, the opportunity to shape the next phase of growth has already passed. In these cases, I have observed that teams and leaders alike forget to check in with themselves and discover whether they can envision themselves in a new future. And from there, find and create new opportunities to contribute in meaningful ways.

When leadership doesn't move with clarity, neither will the business. Busyness without strategic direction creates waste. Busyness without openness stifles growth. And busyness for the sake of management drowns organizations in process rather than progress. But the most difficult challenge? When a business lacks a spine, its leadership fails to make decisions and face risks; it takes steps that are unsupported by conviction and values. Every business has moments of uncertainty. But when leadership hesitates—not because it is weighing options, but because it is avoiding decisions, the entire organization will feel it.

GENERATING FORWARD MOVEMENT

There is no perfect recipe for success, but understanding past wins and what caused them, along with a drive to continuously learn, can improve your momentum. Becoming a leader who drives forward movement requires seeing and *visioning* opportunities, giving oxygen to learning and *expanding* into possibilities, wisely *steering* the business, and standing strong to *embody* and make change materialize.

This book is about ambition and strategy—about seeing higher and making wiser and better choices for you and your business. But strategy is not just about making a long list of choices—it is a dynamic force shaped by how we perceive, adapt, take action, and stand with resilience. It is not about having all the answers but about creating the right conditions for success. It is about developing the capability to place each new piece of the puzzle as it emerges. My intent is not to provide a conclusive view or a thorough diagnostic. Instead, consider this an invitation to reflect, strengthen, and expand wherever you feel you are not set up for success yet. Through sharing my admittedly subjective experiences with you, I wish to challenge your perspectives, respectfully provoke, complement with knowledge, and equip you to be a better version of yourself. My experiences are, by nature, subjective, and shared with a focus on which elements seem most effective for learning rather than a comprehensive and detailed view of the situation.

In today's world, strategy cannot exist in isolation from technology. It is a driving force—one that not only creates possibilities but also exposes misalignment. That is why it is woven into discussions on leadership, consumers, and teams, not as a separate topic, but as a fundamental part of business. Companies don't need standalone digital or tech strategies—there should be only one strategy, and everything must contribute to it. Yet, despite significant investments, many businesses struggle to see impact, while tech companies continue to widen the profit gap. Success is not about adopting technology for its own sake but about integrating it as a core enabler. Those who do will lead—not just keep up.

This book is about empowering you with the four forces that drive business forward:

1. Visioning: The lens through which we see the future determines how we shape it. Clarity of vision allows for bold, deliberate movement rather than reactive stumbling.

2. Expanding: Just as deep breath fuels endurance, expansive thinking oxygenates transformation, allowing organizations to stretch beyond old constraints and accelerate momentum.

3. Steering: Transformation is about active change. Skilled hands don't just grasp opportunities, they sculpt direction, refining rough ideas into deliberate action. They also reach out to bring people along.

4. Embodying: True transformation happens from within. It's not about standing still but about having the spine to stand strong while adapting with agility and embodying conviction to create followership.

These forces are not theoretical concepts—they come from lived experience. They influence how change takes hold, how businesses create impact, and how leaders bring others with them. This book explores how to harness them effectively to drive real, lasting, and meaningful change.

Transformation isn't just about the business: It starts with the leader. The journeys of business and personal growth are deeply intertwined. Leaders who recognize that the organization's transformation must start with their own are set up for success. Those who don't risk wasting resources and draining those around them with efforts that ultimately won't stick. Any investment made into a business's transformation ahead of personal development is likely not to deliver a return on investment (ROI). Whereas, if you are open to developing yourself and leading with this awareness, your business mind will grow sharper, and your business will become more successful.

Personally, I have always been one to see further. *Envisioning* has always come naturally to me. I was born curious and quickly recognized how changing the context could entirely redefine the value of your capabilities, creating new possibilities. It became clear to me that shifting perspective gives you the power of choice.

> **Leaders who recognize that the organization's transformation must start with their own are set up for success.**

Expansive thinking has always mattered to me, but in the past, I didn't always create space for it in others. I used to wait for people to prove their worth before giving them space to inspire. Over time, though, countless small moments challenged my perspective, and I realized that being open is essential to driving success. Now, I lead with that belief—and I'm proud of it.

Steering, rolling up my sleeves to demonstrate, prove, and invite others into a different result has been a part of my entire life. Once I recognized the potential, it felt like a missed opportunity not to test the hypothesis by driving focused effort and passion to see what real value could emerge.

Embodied strength was the last piece to truly click for me. I had read the memos, trained for it, and clearly identified how others struggled as they searched for an external compass. I had seen it happen repeatedly but failed to recognize it in myself. Others saw it in me first, but only once I had fully embodied it did I grasp its true role in orchestrating change. I had long known that the opposite of soft isn't hard but strong. But being both the mast and the sail—each essential for movement—required my full conviction.

You will have your own journey into this. For some, steering may feel obvious, seeing further may seem abstract, and connecting with how you lead with strength may at first appear irrelevant. But having witnessed a significant amount of change throughout my career, I know the results speak for themselves. Understanding how to recognize and apply these underlying forces to both your leadership and your business will drive the success of both.

PART I

....

VISIONING

The lens through which you see the future determines how you shape it. Clarity of vision allows for bold, deliberate movement rather than reactive stumbling.

1

DECODING THE FUTURE
THROUGH STRATEGIC INSIGHT

Adapting to change is no longer enough—as leaders we must learn to read ahead. Industries converge, technologies disrupt, and consumer expectations evolve at an unrelenting pace. We are witnessing the rise of streaming services, the software-defined vehicles revolutionizing the automotive industry, and countless other examples. Those who wait to react will always be a step behind. Leaders who cling to the status quo risk obsolescence.

To thrive in this ever-shifting environment, the key is to seek new knowledge and challenge your own assumptions. The ability to read ahead, discern emerging patterns, and adapt accordingly is no longer a luxury but a necessity. To look ahead isn't just about keeping up with the present but about developing the foresight to identify emerging shifts before they fully take hold. Pattern recognition comes from actively engaging with diverse inputs—studying how medical researchers spot anomalies in patient data, how financial analysts detect shifts in market behavior, or how historians trace the emergence of social movements. It involves scanning across industries, drawing from fields such as neuroscience, urban planning, or consumer psychology, and researching technological breakthroughs that may at first seem unrelated. This requires stepping beyond immediate concerns and drawing from innovations outside of your own industry. The ability to connect these varied insights will enable you to anticipate where value is shifting and make informed, strategic decisions before the market fully pivots. Those who cultivate this ability don't just react to change—they stay ahead of it.

FORCES SHAPING THE FUTURE

As leaders we all keep up with the news on some level. Yet even that reinforces existing perceptions. In light of my experience leading global businesses for companies headquartered in California, London, Paris, and Copenhagen, I can for sure say that being "global" means looking out across a wider scene from your own vantage point. How far you see and with which lens is clearly influenced by this, but global is still a result of your subjective lens and outsets. Even global news outlets have versions adapted to what they believe is most wanted, and here I am only using geography as a symbol for a frame with which one sees. How about different ideologies? Different business models? Different delivery horizons? How often have you for instance asked ChatGPT, Gemini, or Google to share news from another angle? Have you actively forced it to place you in a poorly funded but brilliantly clever underdeveloped market, for instance?

The ability to step beyond your default frame of reference is not just an intellectual exercise—it is a leadership necessity. Leading a strategic business transformation team across industries was an incredibly powerful experience for me. One day, I had to think like an attorney general overseeing national data security. The next, I stepped into the mindset of a CFO managing the financial strategy of an insurance company. Understanding their position, their challenges, and my proposition within their realities was interesting, valuable, and always worthwhile.

It was not as hard as most people perceive it to be, and it did not take much time. But it did take conscious effort. Not only will it allow you to meet people where they are and build value for them, but organizations that recognize emerging trends and have the flexibility to adapt strategies when needed possess a distinct advantage: the capacity to not only react to change but take an active role in shaping it.

Despite the flood of information you face as a leader, it's easy to mistake noise for insight. With constant technological advancements and market shifts demanding your attention, it's tempting to equate speed of response with foresight. But shaping the future isn't about reacting the fastest—it's about seeing beyond the obvious signals to recognize deeper shifts before they become unavoidable. Your job isn't to chase every trend; it's to understand the undercurrents that reveal where value is headed next.

One of those undercurrents is the evolution of language. While the hype of "metaverse" or "Web3" may long have been deemed overrated by the public, the underlying ideas—connecting and exchanging beyond the physical world and enabling decentralized data structures and digital ecosystems—continue to shape technological and business developments. The terminology may fade, but the shifts remain. This is why curiosity matters: not because of the words but because of what they signal.

These shifts rarely start in the mainstream. Instead, they emerge at the fringes—within subcultures, niche communities, and early adopters who experiment with new ideas long before they become part of the broader market. Cryptocurrency was once confined to online forums before it disrupted finance. Social platforms that now define communication started as underground networks. What may seem distant or niche today often serves as a preview of what industries will face tomorrow. Cultivating a sensitivity to "weak signals" and anomalies above averages is also how you can best become curious about patterns without chasing every small opportunity out there.

A customer who previously only bought finished products enquiring about raw material pricing may be a random ask, but if it happens at the same time that trade barriers are set up in a market holding a large part of a supply chain—that is a signal. Or rather it should be. Too often it is not. The number of companies who wait until external parties such as governments, regulators, or competitors set the boundaries before they act is staggering. When we as business leaders neglect to see signals that are showing in our own data, we end up making decisions under time pressure and alongside everyone else, rather than positioning ourselves ahead of the shift and building for optionality.

If you foster a mindset attuned to these subtle cues, you will gain an edge in anticipating and responding to unforeseen challenges and opportunities. By actively incorporating unconventional predictors, you won't just solve today's challenge but also develop a broader understanding of the forces shaping the future and navigate transformations with greater confidence and foresight.

THE RESPONSIBILITY TO SHAPE TOMORROW

I once presented to a set of public healthcare professionals who were guiding and setting standards for hospitals on AI. In the audience were hospital owners, directors, managers, and senior doctors. We exchanged information and had a good debate until a doctor said that, while he intellectually understood it, he was not going to engage. He shared that he had a great X-ray machine. He used software from a partner he had trusted his entire career and believed they were doing adequate upgrades on their software for him to continue using it as his decision partner. I asked him whether he ever debated his diagnosis with anyone, and he shared that when in doubt, he relied on trusted colleagues he would call in. I asked if he ever gave any of this feedback to the company providing the X-ray software and recommendations. The answer was no. It was clear that not only did he believe that he (and whoever was physically close to him at the moment of need) had all the answers, or at least enough, but he also showed no interest in helping the world grow smarter from his expertise.

Letting knowledge remain siloed in people's heads and allowing processes to be defined solely by static software created by external vendors who do not have daily interactions inherently limits growth. Not only does this slow down learning and development for everyone, but on an individual level, it also increases the risk of becoming redundant—in more ways than one.

The latest advancements in AI and increased access to adaptive, collaborative technologies shift both the possibilities and the responsibilities for professionals. The reluctance of the senior doctor to dialogue with AI in human language—to share his insights and learn from broader professional expertise—meant that he missed the opportunity to guide and learn from evolving AI capabilities. Relying solely on static, predefined systems reflects a mindset rooted in comfort rather than progress.

AI algorithms have already demonstrated their transformative potential in healthcare, surpassing traditional benchmarks and enhancing precision. For example, some of the latest models not only exceed the medical licensing exam pass marks but continue to improve with further training. According to internal company data, while traditional systems in 2023 typically considered an average of twenty-seven data points for a diagnosis, AI models launched at that time evaluated approximately 150,000 variables, leading to significant advancements such as a 27 percent reduction in unnecessary hospitalizations.[1] This is not about replacing human expertise but augmenting it—offering more holistic, data-driven insights to healthcare professionals.

Two important considerations emerge: First, doctors with a solid base of medical knowledge can make a powerful contribution to AI systems by continuously broadening the data and refining its recommendations. This works much like when someone searches on Google and clicks a relevant link, strengthening the underlying algorithm's effectiveness over time. Second, limiting input to a small, select group of professionals risks biases and inadequate coverage of diverse healthcare needs. Widespread, inclusive input ensures the data guiding AI solutions is robust and globally relevant. If only a few voices shape these systems, biases will be reinforced, creating risks in critical sectors such as healthcare. As in all others.

The doctor I met was reliant on his machine and the software he had become accustomed to using. Just like many other great wheels of society, this one is run by the cogs of systems and processes, steered by those who paid to make it easier for users to follow. Or, said differently, the bulk of our world is run by software shaped in the 1990s or 2000s, so relying on the processes served keeps you anchored in the software assumptions of that time.[2]

This is not a blame game or a call to push responsibility to one player versus another but a call for all to reflect on the responsibility and value exchanged. In this case, the provider of the X-ray machine may not even be aware of how a simple conversational AI and vision AI could help them gather input from all their machines and, from that, create a learning network that would, in turn, enable any active player to continuously learn from every engagement. If the provider of the X-ray machine was not willing to make it worth the doctors' while and let them feed back into the machine, they would be holding the sector back. They would, with time, become less trustworthy as a source of recommendation as to what is right for the patient. The sad part here is that it would take time, which also means that today there are many areas of business where a narrow mindset is both limiting development and resulting in those with the expertise not being part of shaping the future. We should all have an interest in combining quantitative insights with qualitative expertise to arrive at the best decisions.

But when it comes to defining "best," is that ever truly straightforward? Is it longevity? Speed of treatment? Or even, dare I say, the commercial success of a particular remedy? The reality is that different stakeholders—patients, doctors, researchers, and businesses—each view the same information through their own lens. Defining the future may be impossible; however, recognizing these competing perspectives is not just about ethical decision-making. It is about seeing the full picture and understanding how different vantage points are likely to try to shape the future. Doing nothing, on the other hand, will only mean that someone else will decide what defines the future. While this doctor's experience may represent a specific challenge within the healthcare industry, it reflects a broader truth about business change. The frame through which we choose to look defines the ceiling of our success.

In many ways, I first shaped this skill when I started my career and was defining the next decade for century-old brands at Moet Hennessy and Diageo, only to be further accelerated by today's pace of change and opportunity. I share this because being entrusted early on with the huge legacies of brands that have set new horizons and survived all kinds of changes reminded me that it is not the moment in time that defines you; it is about how you make the most of the chapter you have been asked to write.

> **The frame through which we choose to look defines the ceiling of our success.**

When I was leading a global industry for Google and engaging with several of the largest leaders in that sector, the ability to imagine and simulate the future—and challenge them to reflect on their role within it—was essential. They were curious about each other, but by focusing efforts on looking wider at their collective future, space was created for many to grow simultaneously. Rather than waiting for the landscape to change, they leaned into where they had a chance to excel, and together we managed to double our growth.

When we partnered with multiple businesses in the same industry, it was, of course, essential to understand what was considered differentiating and proprietary. Therefore, from technology conversations, we swiftly moved to strategy conversations and then to identity conversations. Only this way could we identify what would quickly become industry norms and where our partners should bet their innovations. Take, for instance, the ability to converse with systems: It is now a basic function—something that wasn't possible just a few years ago. The same goes for converting documents to digital formats, searching internal company information, or seamlessly ingesting public data that affects business decisions. Each of these capabilities was once out of reach. Today, they are readily available to us all. Think about choose as capabilities that allow you to accelerate the next chapter of your business's destiny, not be the destiny or hold you to existing processes while someone else shapes the future of your industry and takes your future value.

So when I advise executives today, one part is always addressed: understanding where the space around you is headed and defining an ambition within it before we start building with intention. The question is no longer *if* they can be leveraged but *how* they will be integrated to drive progress. One of the most fatal mistakes I experience some leaders make is limiting the lens through which they see their market and potential. If instead you step back and reflect on your company's role and value today, is it reflecting the opportunities around you? Or just maintaining the status quo?

Those who have grown up in tech always laugh about this example, but for the majority of people I have shared it with, it has been helpful. If you are the same generation as I am, you likely grew up with a large rack of CDs. They were the quality delivery of the music you wanted. We had carefully selected and invested in albums and had our favorite bands' music in our rooms. But then came iTunes. And the overwhelming joy we experienced at the convenience of being able to not only bring our whole music catalogs with us but also access them across multiple devices. It felt like a huge breakthrough. Also, it was clear that from a commercial standpoint, iTunes kept us loyal—as some would say, "locked in"—because when we had all our music there, we would think twice before buying other products. It was now no longer only about the device but also about the access to our own content. But today, we live in a world of Spotify. We have access to all music, we expect to get relevant recommendations, and we expect to be able to share and jam with those in our network. This is clearly not just about music. The world is moving from siloed experiences to connected experiences to predictive experiences. Consumers have already made the shift, and human habits are moving this way, too, yet leadership behavior is still often operating as if we all still buy CDs.

VALUE REDISTRIBUTION

When I use the CD, iTunes, or Spotify example, someone always says that this has been the worst thing for the creators of the valuable asset (the music), as they no longer get the same income from this. Or they talk about how airlines were part of dragging value out of their own industry when they formed the standard-setting trade association IATA and supported Sabre (created by one airline) and Amadeus (created by four others). But what we need to recognize is that the value does not go away; it is just redistributed. The value in these instances went to the users and a select number of businesses who used data to show the users value. And now with AI models available for businesses and industries to tune to specific business needs, leaders across all industries must grapple with this challenge. This is not just about using AI. It is about innovating with and building with AI. Because value isn't destroyed by disruption, it simply shifts. The question for us as leaders becomes, "Who captures that shifting value?"

During my executive career, I was on the decision panel for a gigantic IT implementation. We represented a significant player in a very consolidated market, or, said differently, the provider of this specific piece of tech had very few potential customers. The software company was well respected across multiple fields but had built this industry solution with one of our largest competitors and was now keen to get us on board. For sure there would be fast value once deployed and the many hours they had spent building it would come in handy. However, there were some fundamental elements that made me a strong opponent of the pitch.

First, in an industry where there are so few players, the value of getting a second significant player on board would cement the value to them in the market, and therefore they would be able to sell to others. So, in my mind, they should be paying us for the implementation. Second, as this was not an industry where market dynamics had driven standardization, the insights of a second customer would be so valuable for them for future development. So, while I could recognize the convenience of us taking the software, I believed that the tradeoff was that, at that point in time, the value for the software company was greater than it would be for us. I stayed opposed, and more joined this camp for various reasons. It did not go through, despite huge political debate. The CIO left the company over this decision. It is now many years later, and the software company has since stopped supporting the product. In fact, even the industrial company with which they built it has stopped using it, with both companies losing millions of dollars on this initiative. Some people in this process had far deeper knowledge of the business and systems than I did. However, their proximity to the details prevented them from stepping back and seeing the potential of the bigger picture.

A sector I have also been fortunate to partner with is the automobile industry. It is a great illustration of change. Some might argue that the biggest shift has been driven by the move to electrification, followed by an increased global competition from the stronger presence of Chinese manufacturers versus the US Midwest players and long-established European businesses. While autonomous driving has largely remained a distant concept for many, elements of it have quietly entered the market through assisted driving features—acting as a kind of trojan horse to something we will probably see in full form sooner rather than later. Meanwhile, advancements in in-vehicle technology, infotainment, and customer experience have been welcomed and appreciated by users.

However, I believe that one key lever is the most strategically interesting one to learn from: the shift to software-defined vehicles.

In car companies, historically, engineering has been driving the direction. New cars were added based on engineering competences; designers did their touches, and consumers were given options to configure their cars with engine sizes, colors, stitches, and all kinds of hidden technical rewards. But the complexity did not match the value. The automakers were left with extreme costs to manage manufacturing and stock. The cost of the value chain and dealers handling this was unnecessary, and the increasing power of fleet management companies obscured the picture even more. What has shifted this was most publicly introduced by Tesla. They took a digital mindset and brought it into the manufacturing world and were able to significantly shift the margins. It's worth remembering that learning isn't only about the stories we admire. Understanding what strengthened positions—regardless of who led them—is what teaches us the most.

They looked at the market and data and, from that, identified grouped needs. They saw a need for two models, brought these to market, and did not ask whether people wanted a hundred different configuration models. They used data as input, not as the answer. This meant they were able to triple the margin compared to leading players in the industry. Their cars became the starting point for engagement, not the end goal. Just like iPhones, where no two devices are used the same even though we all purchase the same hardware, Tesla knew that they could take the physical part of the auto industry and make it into just the foundation, building on top of it from there with technology and software. Since then, companies such as Mercedes have also proclaimed that, while maintaining their strong engineering, the focus and investment will be on building experiences and a quality luxury feel—or, as it was said, to become the "Hermès of automotive." But today, a large part of the automotive industry is struggling because they had not thought ahead and planned for this. Now they are trying to shape both a product and an identity in light of a changing context.

And this is where understanding the maturity of industries becomes crucial. Consider the historical parallels: Just like building physical infrastructure such as roads, ports, and distribution networks provided access to customers and fueled growth going into this century, telco businesses had an era of reward for their investments in the networks, and both are now clinging onto value while actively investing to expand beyond this. The same pattern is unfolding today with AI infrastructure. The race to build computing power, data pipelines, and scalable models is similar to the early days of telco and transportation. But just as we've seen in other industries, those investing in AI today will eventually either move into another investment group or choose to go beyond infrastructure and rethink how intelligence is applied to create real advantage.

But having the infrastructure is not the same as knowing how to use it effectively. The doctor's reluctance to engage with AI was not due to a lack of understanding but because of a hesitation to expand his remit. The automotive industry now faces a similar reckoning. Technology and infrastructure are available to them; however, this alone does not secure relevance. What matters is looking wider, reading the seismic shifts, and leading your business to see, select, and engage with new possibilities before it is too late.

Success belongs not to those who digitize the past but to those who anticipate the future and recognize opportunities for value redistribution. It is not about merely keeping pace; it is about recognizing how value migrates and positioning accordingly. Businesses that thrive are not just upgrading their systems; they are seeing further and deploying wisely. Most leaders today understand that transformation is not driven by technology alone—it is shaped by mindset. But the real challenge is recognizing that this mindset is not just about being curious about technology. It is also about being curious about the world and where it is headed, with technology as an enabler. For some this may be reassuring, as it builds on a familiar skill set rather than requiring a completely new one. For others, it may serve as a reminder that the ability to see where a business can grow is not a static skill—it must be continuously sharpened to stay ahead. It requires a willingness to step outside your comfort zone and challenge your long-held assumptions. It is about having the curiosity, adaptability, and foresight to move before the market does. The companies that reshape industries are the ones that engage with change before it becomes urgent.

True disruption comes from those who leverage that presence to cultivate a deep understanding of their users and translate that understanding into exceptional value. Ultimately, the challenges faced by organizations reflect the mindset of their leaders. The need to confront change applies not just to systems and processes but to personal growth and willingness to challenge established practices. This requires that you take a proactive approach to understanding the subtle forces shaping the future and move beyond simply reacting to the known market—instead, actively seeking out the less obvious indicators of change.

2

LEADING WITH CONVICTION AND EXPLORATION

S eeing wider enables you to see ahead. Seeing faster enables you to win. With all the possibilities available to us, how do we as leaders or executives turn potential into business value without simultaneously shutting down what has just been opened up? The challenge is not just about recognizing opportunities—it's about choosing a method that enables high ambitions and continuous contributions toward them.

Consider the numbers: McKinsey and BCG both cite transformation failure rates at around 70 percent,[1] while Bain & Co. claims 88 percent.[2] At the same time, firms like McKinsey and EY highlight significant and impressive potential ROI of successful AI implementations.[3] Despite longstanding awareness of transformation challenges and past waves of technology promises, few organizations have developed the capability to balance transformation with tangible ROI. The disconnect between talk and execution is real. Yet, while there are more stories of failure than success, there are clear patterns that lead to sustainable change.

Recognizing potential and setting a direction doesn't mean having all the answers. In today's fast-moving landscape, progress comes less from maintaining control and more from enabling targeted exploration. As leaders, we have grown up in a world where our job was to control—to control the direction, the resources, and the movement toward the goal we have set. Most corporations that define our world today were built in the decades when hierarchies thrived, strategies were created with highly paid external consultants, and projects involved stage gates, waterfall planning, and steering committees. For middle management and junior executives, that meant learning the timing of budget cycles by heart and navigating endless bureaucracy, all within a system that structurally is built more to maintain than to change. I have seen many employees live with the binary status afforded to them. Either they were respected and therefore had to run the business while finding time to share input on every major project, or they were endlessly waiting for the green light from those budget cycles.

Then came the Era of Agile. The new black. The thing that would deliver bigger and better results at a faster pace while empowering the team. Scrum masters were the new heroes, and every morning you could hear a chorus of high-fives given around dashboards to celebrate small wins. It was originally created in reaction to the many projects that ran over budget and time. A team of experienced software developers created a manifesto that focused on individuals and interactions, customer collaboration, and responding to change over following a plan. Unfortunately, it has not always been applied as intended, and I have seen all too many businesses where nonengineering teams have created small islands of hype—good or bad—that are all too often not adequately connected to larger organizational change.

The debate between building long-term strategic plans and adopting an agile mindset often mirrors the differences between start-ups and corporates. If you, like me, have worked with both, you know that neither has the perfect formula for success. Start-ups thrive on speed and adaptability but often struggle when they reach the point where structure and scalability becomes necessary. Corporates, on the other hand, may have the resources and market presence, but they also carry the weight of bureaucracy, making it difficult to move with the same agility.

Internal ventures, or intrapreneurship, promise the best of both worlds: corporate backing with entrepreneurial freedom. In theory, everyone supports the idea of innovation from within, but in practice, it is rarely as seamless as one might expect. More than once, I have seen corporate start-ups dismissed as "kindergartens with trust funds"— protected but not always taken seriously. At the same time, these ventures face real constraints. Seeking external funding can be more difficult because of corporate ownership, and while customers respect the backing of a large company, they often expect a different level of service, speed, and flexibility than the corporate machine typically allows. These tensions can feel frustrating, but they also hold valuable lessons for leadership. At Google, even within an innovative culture versus the market average, the consequence was taken to develop a moonshot factory, Google X, a separate entity that operates on different terms, timelines, and structures, with the goal of incubating breakthrough technologies that can eventually become independent businesses or be integrated into Google's existing products and services. Holding this dual path forward both gives space for grander innovations and also demands strong leadership to ensure optimal contribution of the radical discoveries to Google's strategic ambitions.

The key is not just creating space for innovation but leading it with conviction. Intrapreneurship works when leaders set a clear direction and ensure alignment on ambition—and when contribution toward the goal is valued and respected equally by both the innovating and the standing parts of the business.

Past methodologies commonly called for setting a goal and evaluating against that,

Venturing defines a strategic direction and focuses all efforts on courageous exploration of new territories.

whether long-term or short-term. However, with the pace of change—especially now with AI selectively accelerating—unfortunately, this is insufficient. What I have seen succeed is the concept of venturing. Venturing defines a strategic direction and focuses all efforts on courageous exploration of new territories to drive growth, value, and competitive advantage in pursuit of the set ambition. It is a clear articulation of the role the business aims to play in the market or society and ideally to avoid aimless exploration, with a focus on the audience to be served. It is inspired by, but not the same as, venture capital or corporate venturing—this isn't about funding experiments but about committing the full business to explore and shape the space it chooses to play in. It is not an EBITDA (earnings before interest, taxes, depreciation, and amortization) target or a market goal. It is not a share price target. Most importantly, the steps toward that ambition are *not* predetermined. This gives space for unpredicted contributions yet all with clear impact on the agreed ambition. It also means that pace cannot be predetermined. When applied correctly, this doesn't slow operations down but, rather, speeds up the workflow, because of the healthy competitiveness of ambitious teams striving for new heights. Accountability for progress is shared, with team leaders holding the added responsibility of distributing learnings across the business, ensuring that each step forward builds on the latest insights.

Venturing must, naturally, be aligned with the majority shareholders of the company. Without this alignment, efforts will be wasted. Too often, I have met executives dreaming of bold ambitions, only to discover that those to whom they must report their progress are not ready to enable such an exponential form of growth.

To some, this may sound like a company purpose. In a few instances, I have seen purpose statements that could take on the role of ambition in venturing; however, most purposes today do not adequately connect with market opportunities and needs and, therefore, do not naturally create a sense of direction, guardrails, or what will deliver commercial success for a business.

When the ambition is clear and the reward is shared, the desire to bring the best contributions appeals to a positive drive instead of one where winning requires someone else to lose. Venturing is both winning and reaching further *together*.

OWNING THE PRESENT TO SHAPE THE FUTURE

In one of my executive roles, I was once preparing for a board meeting. I had put together content to share lots of insightful, honest, and deep challenges holding back progress for the business. There were no questions on the validity of the message, but it was a very different style from what had previously been shown to the board. My direct stakeholder, the CCO, was evaluating our recommendation and decided to call the CEO into the room to confirm that the message was board-appropriate. The CEO listened to the content quietly and then asked softly, "Can you take me through it again?" Following the second review, he looked the CCO in the eye and said respectfully, "You know, this happened on our watch. Sharing this could get us fired." He then asked for reflection time. Half an hour later, he returned and confirmed that it was the right thing to do. Not all CEOs, CCOs, and teams have the courage to face such moments proactively. Following the initial board shock, the conversation deepened. What followed was not defensiveness, but a constructive dialogue about how past priorities had affected customers—and what needed to change moving forward. This board meeting was a defining moment in the company's transformation. From there, a more conscious and balanced approach of leveraging customer feedback loops started to future-proof the business. It not only set a new, clear direction forward but also demonstrated a leadership approach in which development areas were owned, and the board reaffirmed its commitment to the CEO's leadership. This level of alignment and accountability is essential for driving leadership during times of change.

When visionary Howard Schultz decided to position Starbucks as "a third place" between home and work, a concept originated by sociologist

Ray Oldenburg,[4] it felt incredibly ambitious but has since become exactly that for many. He did not, at that time, have all the network of stores, staffing, loyalty programs, or a global brand in place. What he had was conviction in a goal and invited others to contribute toward it.

Similarly, in the 1990s, Richard Branson applied a form of venturing by expanding Virgin beyond its origins as a record label into businesses diverse enough to encompass airlines, mobile communication, and financial services—all united by a conviction that an experience-driven philosophy could redefine industries.

Both Howard Schultz and Richard Branson faced significant stakeholder challenges in bringing their ambitions to life, yet their success came from how they engaged resistance, aligned others with their vision, and navigated skepticism without losing conviction. Instead of focusing on objections as obstacles, Schultz demonstrated the emotional and social value of his vision, proving its impact step by step. Branson, by contrast, was bolder in his approach by entering industries where incumbents saw him as an outsider, positioning Virgin as a challenger that broke through inefficiencies and outdated norms. Both stories have ample learning to offer. Starbucks's financial performance stands as a clear model of sustained success driven by strong conviction. Virgin's expansive ambition created a unique advantage—opening doors to industries others wouldn't dare to enter and fostering a culture of continuous reinvention. Though some ventures thrived while others struggled, Branson's businesses generated billions in revenue and his approach cemented Virgin's identity as a fearless innovator, proving that challenging convention can be a strategic asset in itself.

Schultz and Branson both understood that conviction alone is not enough—engagement, proactive alignment, and strategic proof points are what turn resistance into momentum. This is what sets great leaders apart in times of transformation. Those who reframe objections to find common ground, engage critical voices early to preempt pitfalls, and establish clear leading indicators, create the conditions for success. Whether that means proving the Starbucks experience store by store or showing that a Virgin airline could compete on service and efficiency, these leaders understood that the right metrics, the right conversations, and the right narrative can build belief even among skeptics. Effective stakeholder alignment is both welcoming contributions toward the ambition and recognizing that the immediate desire for clarity is not always the real issue so much as a habit. As effective leaders and executives, we must go beyond surface-level objections to uncover the underlying hesitations, transforming concerns into opportunities for clarity, alignment, and sustainable progress.

THE POWER OF KNOWING AND UNKNOWING

Venturing with a clear ambition invites exploration and allows parallel teams to work on the same challenge. When I joined Google some years ago, I had come from an executive role in a traditional global industrial player—a forward-thinking and ambitious company where all the latest leadership training had been made available and the company had invested in our growth. I thought I was informed about the latest exponential thinking. What I knew was not incorrect, but the degree of forward thinking I encountered at Google blew me away.

As I was doing my round of introductions, I met a team who explained the very specific challenge they were solving. A few days later, I had the exact same conversation with a completely different team. My previous role had been for a low-margin business, so my first instinct was to drive efficiency by only having one team focused on the task and reassigning the other team. I was wrong. Following my initial surprise, I politely asked whether the two teams worked together, but as it turned out, they were not even aware of each other. I found myself in the unusual position, a few days into my role, of introducing the two teams to each other. Later, I spoke to a seasoned Googler (name for an employee at Google), told him the story, and asked for cultural insights on how to handle the situation. He explained that for Google, the situation was by design. As nobody knew which of the two teams would succeed, it would be wrong to force them together and anchor their thinking too closely, potentially stifling innovation. They were, of course, welcome to connect and share, but if the same frame and input were considered by both teams, it would narrow their mindset. So, to my great surprise, they met, they chatted, and they became friends, but they continued working independently for a long time. Eventually, one team reached a breakthrough and went down the path to productization, whereas the other team had taken some turns, and their learnings ended up as a feature in another core Google offering. No one could have predicted this.

This approach represents an ideology and a mindset. While many will immediately see the cost incurred, I hope it equally provokes an awareness of how many strong ideas may never see the light of day. And where the cost of duplicate teams may be easy to quantify, the value of finding the best solution will inevitably be harder to predict and calls for a shift in leadership approach, moving from a traditional command-and-control style to one that embraces empowerment and focuses on venturing ambitiously in the direction of the course.

During my time at Google, I once found myself in a closed-door meeting with some of the country's top industrial leaders in this G7 economy, which made it crystal clear that awareness is not always the only barrier. The discussion for the day? Whether they were willing to trust cloud providers with their most critical operations. I had a brief presentation, the message of which had been pre-approved by three partners and every angle had been tested to ensure compliance. The session went well, and the tenured host smiled and nodded at my every message. A livelier Q&A followed. The audience was engaged, asking questions they did otherwise not dare, questioning motivations, growth strategies, and ambitions. It was a good conversation. They understood the value and the potential and had a fair assessment of what was needed to mitigate the risks they saw. The meeting finished, they clapped, and I was thanked and politely asked to leave. As I walked out with a clear sense that this had been an educational yet not transformational meeting for any of them, a prominent leader among the group got up to walk me out of the room. He thanked me for the discussion and said quietly, "You know, it all makes sense, and the value could be huge for us to steer our expertise into this future, but the reality is, all of us have three to seven years left in our careers, and it is better to hold a steady ship. We can achieve more for sure by leveraging this potential, but we don't *have* to, and the risk is big that we will personally fail."

I went back and forth on being encouraged or discouraged by the room that day. It was great they had reached an understanding and made a conscious decision based on the information available. However, the decision was also influenced by fear and a mindset rooted in either outdated thinking or, at best, maintaining the status quo. As a result, it did not position their businesses or teams for a significant role in the future of their industry. Mostly, I am surprised because I know for a fact that these leaders—and many like them—are investing resources and have talented teams eager to make a transformative change. Yet the real challenge lies in leadership taking an active role and ensuring that contributions are not only encouraged but fully enabled, while also being forthright about real constraints so they can be addressed together.

VENTURING WITH CONVICTION

By its very nature, venturing into new territory, setting ambitious goals, and encouraging contributions toward them will move the business forward with each step. Yet by the nature of it, no one can predict in advance exactly how fast and where it will land. But when we as leaders live this approach, it becomes transformational, and the lessons learned along the way serve to accelerate every step.

One leadership story that stands out as a strong inspiration is that of Luca de Meo. When de Meo joined Groupe Renault as CEO, the company had a solid operation and was primarily known for its French mid-market brand. At Google, I was privileged to partner with this company, which proved to be far more dynamic and forward-thinking than initial perceptions suggested, demonstrating a bold approach to innovation and transformation. However, they were struggling to make a significant impact on the global car market. At the time, the auto industry was experiencing a shift toward electrification, and the first signs of software-defined vehicles were emerging. Beyond commercial interests, Groupe Renault also held a societal responsibility to protect local jobs while navigating real limitations on customer investment potential.

De Meo's response was "Renaulution"[5]—a great strategy driven not by emotion but by a clear assessment of the company's position. He demonstrated an impressive ability to recognize areas where Renault might struggle to lead while simultaneously identifying opportunities for growth in ways that were not immediately obvious.

The partnership with Google provided valuable insights into Renault's operations but naturally offered only a limited view of the company's internal decision-making. Nonetheless, Luca de Meo's leadership serves a compelling case study in transformation—one where strategy is rooted in realism yet boldly dares to push beyond the traditional thinking of the automotive industry.

For instance, de Meo's focus was not just on Renault's immediate performance but on fundamentally reshaping how the company could thrive in an evolving market. A business that had historically managed brands now took a bolder leap to give much more distinctive positions to those brands. But even more interestingly, he also split out engines and electrification as businesses, to serve not just his own market but also the wider market. So instead of taking a backseat in supply lines, he was able to turn strategy into purchasing power and position Renault in more layers of this evolving market.

By empowering the organization to challenge some of the previously held holy grails, they quickly were able to limit the range of models, paradoxically enabling a more competitive position. By streamlining the lineup, Renault was able to overcome the challenge of long lead times that typically plague car manufacturers. This was an innovative way of creating efficiency while also positioning the company to be more agile in responding to market demands. All while the teams were able to reduce cost of inventory holdings.

Additionally, de Meo saw the need to challenge the traditional retail model, advocating for closer engagement with consumers. His teams understood that modern consumers are looking not just for products but for experiences. By getting closer to them, Renault could transform its relationship with the customer, moving beyond just being a supplier of vehicles to becoming a key player in the broader mobility ecosystem.

Another forward-thinking aspect of Renaulution was its take on sustainability. It was not merely about tracking carbon emissions or meeting regulatory targets. Instead, it was about offering customers the chance to refurbish their cars, which created a dual impact: It contributed to environmental goals and helped maintain loyalty and shift consumer behavior. This move nudged a variety of players—from consumers to competitors to regulators—to rethink how the industry could evolve.

What truly set de Meo's work apart was not just the individual initiatives but the volume of transformations in pursuit of an ambition—the momentum created, the invitation for bold ideas, the realistic self-assessment, and the internal restructuring to create a shift that transcended traditional industry norms. With conviction, he ventured into uncharted territory, always keeping an eye on who could accelerate his progress. By breaking his business into building blocks and leveraging data—from consumer insights to supply chain optimization—de Meo positioned Renault to act more decisively. This approach allowed the company to expand its market presence, even competing with major players in Asia and Europe.

What Luca de Meo role-modeled is something very unique in my mind. On a meta-level, what he did was think like a tech company, respecting the engineering nature of the business while still being a marketer at heart. And where the learnings and areas that could be stronger may form a long list, too, this is a great example of how venturing enables you to escape being defined by your past and create value by honestly assessing your core, leading with conviction and exploration. This impressive turnaround has thus far demonstrated a deliberate shift toward higher value operations, refining the business by 40 percent, alongside continued improvement in operating margins, ahead of key industry players and a steady and continued increase in net profit.[6]

Leading in a setting of venturing is a delicate balance of a strong conviction and a respectful openness may seem like herding teams toward a desired direction. Where this may be an unflattering explanation it indeed is exactly what is required, and as leaders we must remember that no one can venture if they are on a leash. The lens through which we see the future determines how we shape it. The challenge is not just about recognizing opportunities—it's about choosing a method that enables high ambitions and continuous contributions toward them.

3

FUTURE-PROOFING PROFIT POOLS

To shape the future of a business beyond a clear vision and stakeholder buy-in, data is often an accelerator. However, digitization is not the finish line. It's simply the starting point for businesses that want to survive, and more importantly, thrive in an AI-driven world. Too many organizations still see digitization as the final destination: converting manual processes into digital formats, automating repetitive tasks, or creating data repositories. If digitization is driven solely by efficiency, businesses risk far more than missed opportunities—they risk irrelevance. Without a clear vision, I have seen too many businesses fail to harness the true power of data and AI to redefine their value propositions and unlock new profit pools. Instead of fueling innovation, investments become short-sighted, leaving the company vulnerable to obsolescence in an era where venturing boldly into the future is the only way to stay ahead.

Many businesses take too binary a view of digitization. They either decide not to as they fear loss of value, or they give it all away. Seeing your businesses through the lens of data gives a deeper understanding and actionable insights—subsequently, giving you the control to decide whether this serves internal products, external products, or maybe even new business models. It is not just about collecting data—it is about understanding what that data reveals and how it can reshape business strategy. This is where too many businesses falter: Data is collected but not interpreted for deeper implications. It is crucial to recognize what is truly at stake with the data you gather.

THE RISK OF ANTIQUATED PROCESSES

In the early years of my career, "digital" was synonymous with website cloning of corporate websites and social media. Fast-forward to around 2015, while I was at Maersk, and conversations had shifted. Conversations about disruption and digitization were largely around e-commerce and blockchain, often sparking polarized camps: those who dismissed them as fads and those who saw the potential to fundamentally change the business. As is often the case, neither extreme was fully true. One camp believed self-serve customer journeys and integrated order handling would be the way to balance better service and lower cost to serve. The other said the industry was not ready. After quite a lot of customer research—both quantitative and qualitative—it was found there was keen interest but little intention to change.

With this new information, the internal debate flourished. The development initiatives got scrutinized and shaved but not killed. Eighteen months later, the customers were able to place orders online and manage more of their journey electronically, and the first application programming interfaces (APIs) ensured two-way communication. At that point the exact same customer research was conducted again, and this time the feedback was unanimously positive. There were ample chances to have killed this initiative and certainly faster ways to reach the goal. But by building ahead of the market, Maersk's platform went on to become among the world's largest websites in terms of revenue, nudging an entire industry into an era of allowing the company to claim a greater share of the business.

Across businesses the number of operations managed through antiquated processes and manual labor is considerable. And while today's digital conversations often center on AI, quantum computing, or what's next in automation, the real connective thread across every wave of disruption is data—how it's captured, understood, and used to make better decisions. If you were building for today or tomorrow, which things would you need? What would your customers and your industry be expecting of you over the next five to ten years? Each wave of change asks something different—not just of our tools but of how we chose to lead.

OWNING THE VALUE OF YOUR DATA

In my extensive work with global enterprises, I have observed a clear pattern: Businesses that strategically outsource their back-end operations to lower-cost partners not only achieve significant cost efficiencies but also successfully unite their teams under consistent standards, something they had previously struggled to accomplish. But what always strikes me as interesting is that the knowledge, the data, and the insights then get placed outside of the core business. While outsourcing can save costs, it can also lead to a loss of control over intellectual property (IP)—particularly the knowledge and insights that could fuel the next big breakthrough.

When you outsource functions that generate a lot of data and insights—for example, customer service and operations—without owning the intellectual property, you inadvertently fund the commoditization of your own business. The data generated, the lessons learned, and the knowledge accumulated over time can become someone else's asset if you are not careful. This is where businesses get stuck—by digitizing without truly understanding the value of the data they're gathering and without taking ownership of the insights that could shape their future. But when you start to see your businesses as a teaching organism—where every experience informs the next decision—you gain a clearer understanding of your own value and what you can contribute to the future market. It's important not to cling to every part of the business simply for the sake of holding on. Instead, viewing your business as a source of data allows you to more easily assess whether what you give away is matched by adequate value in return—whether that value is financial or tied to a future opportunity.

At a recent conference, a well-respected industry leader in financial services proudly talked about how they were using AI through a partner that was trawling through all their data and feeding back recommendations—in other words, he was paying them to use his knowledge to train a sophisticated AI model, which in fact could be more valuable to customers in the future than the package he offered today. He was inadvertently funding the commoditization of his own business. I was listening and honing all my focus to think how I could best—in this very public situation, with all the immense respect I held for him—respectfully alert him of the risk he was taking. I framed the question in a way that was open-ended and curious, yet his sharp mind immediately grasped the underlying point. While he responded with executive poise and politeness, there was no mistaking the speed at which his thoughts were racing beyond the words the audience heard. In that moment, he had just realized the risk. You must be clear about who owns the future value of the data you are generating. What type of relationship do you expect your partners to have in your ecosystem in the future? And what will your role be at that stage?

This point is not a new one. It has always been the case that you can solve for today or prepare for tomorrow, or ideally a bit of both. The difference today is that AI models are more clearly showing the value of learning, as the expertise built up over generations may be determining directions of AI outputs. This is where companies that understand the expertise that has led them to their current positions can be invaluable, and when formatted into data and into AI can secure a strong position in future profit pools. Yet this is also one of those decisions, which, if done wrong, is hard to reverse.

FORTIFYING YOUR VALUE PROPOSITION

Businesses that fail to define what sets them apart risk leaning into AI and diluting the value they have created. Seeing a company's full potential is valuable and exciting, but equally important is the ability to look within. The skill lies in truly understanding what value you hold and must nurture. Fortunately, the skills required for external exploration and visioning are almost the same as those for internal exploration: remaining curious, challenging assumptions, having strategic foresight, and seeing beneath the immediate layers of business.

In branding, as in AI, clarity of essence or core value proposition ensures your ability to play in future value pools. AI tools are available to all. Any business can access information in multiple languages, in any time zone. Any business can open a platform with friendly customer service experience with personalized content experience. So, if you and your competitors all did this at the same time, what would be left for you to win on? Or, said differently, if you were to have access to all the AI models in the world, which would you choose not just to use but to tune with your unique expertise and data?

Opportunity is everywhere—the real skill is discerning which opportunities amplify your essence and which dilute it.

Early in my career, I was in marketing, and I was responsible for some of the most profitable brands in their category. This meant that agencies stood in line to help create the next marketing concepts, and ideas came flying to us from all around the world. It was easy to get excited by talented creatives much like one can be excited by the possibilities of AI. What is powerful about brands that have survived decades is not the volume of opportunities they pursue but the precision with which they chose the ones that reinforce their essence and unique offer.

This awareness is a large part of what enables them to win over time and why marketers hold the responsibility to protect this dearly while ensuring relevance to customers at the time. This is also what defines the ability to charge the premiums that have made the world's luxury companies such as LVMH and L'Oreal among the few who compete with tech executives and top investors on global wealth.[1]

With any number of creative concepts to choose from, if an agency did not enhance and champion our value, it was impossible to even entertain the conversation. If the brand's essence was captured in a compelling idea but lacked the right audience insight or faced execution challenges, we knew it could be refined and improved. Applying the same thinking to AI development means knowing your own core value proposition in order to discern where to be flexible and where to be uncompromising. When executional elements don't define your businesses, you should work with what is available in the market. When something is fundamental to your insights, you must ensure that you leverage only what aligns with your ambitions and your business's core value proposition. Protect it, nurture it, and actively put it to use.

THE NEW GROWTH FRONTIER

Opportunities in innovation and data are galore, yet with the role of businesses in society greatly evolving, maybe another lens should also be applied. Since 2018, public confidence in political institutions has weakened, and eyes have turned toward business leaders to step into roles traditionally reserved for governments. Across the globe, this change is currently fluctuating; however, there is a consistent rise in expectations for senior leaders on social, environmental, and ethical fronts. The 2024 Edelman Trust Barometer highlights trust as a fragile asset and looks for leaders to delicately align technological advancements with societal benefits, manage skepticism, and demonstrate credibility with innovation.[2] Still, trust is often overestimated; 90 percent of executives believe they're trusted, while only 30 percent of consumers agree.[3]

Once again, this offers immense opportunity. For those who wish to lead and are capable of leading, there is huge potential for followership. Companies that engage meaningfully can reshape norms, influence policy, and carve out entirely new markets. But it comes with weight. Done poorly, these efforts can feel hollow or inconsistent, risking credibility and pulling focus away from core business priorities.

Some of the best examples of market creation come from companies that don't just request change but generate enough demand to make the shift worthwhile. For example, simply asking a supplier to modify a product often has little impact. However, when businesses create sufficient demand and commit to meaningful volumes, suppliers see value in adapting—creating a win-win scenario.

During my time at Google, there was a sense of magic that came from the expertise, the culture, and the way of thinking. There was a culture that allowed a very aspirational and inspirational lens on opportunities. They would often approach their own company challenges by asking, "What would Google do?" This thinking is not limited to those who hold positions in the most innovative companies in the world, though. The simple exercise of asking your teams, with or without Google or some other strong player in the room, what would they do? What would Uber do if they owned you? What would your worst competitor do? What would OpenAI do? What would the Chinese government do? What would the Saudi sovereign wealth fund do?

For those who wish to lead and are capable of leading, there is huge potential for followership.

This exercise is not intended to shape a concrete strategy output, but rather to expand minds before sense-checking what is right for you. These exercises are fun, with some teams even wondering if they count as work. But through these conversations, people's minds are opened up, and possibilities arise when unrestrained by internal habits, often revealing the real barriers and underlying drivers. It is a great way to force different thinking. Positioning themselves in another company's frame of reference also removes teams from the initial responsibilities of how to achieve this and fit it into their current workloads. So why should you wait to see where the future brings you when you can leverage your teams in imagining where the future can take you?

Seeing and understanding innovative opportunities paired with societal priorities creates future profit pools. Recognizing when and how these intersect with core business goals is yet another great way to move with a current instead of having to create momentum alone.

BUILDING MOMENTUM

The combination of these increased expectations for business leaders to deliver trust and shape society and a context in which AI is becoming more widely deployed means there is a real opportunity to consciously stand out. Businesses that merely adopt the latest technology risk blending into a sea of sameness, while those that embed it into a distinctive vision, experience, or relationship with their customers create something far more lasting.

It is a shift already experienced in some industries, such as the case with home and beauty products selling popularity rather than functionality. There is nothing blocking them from anticipating consumer needs from patterns of past purchase, scaled through similar personas, connecting this to data from music and streaming platforms to predict their favorite music and stars, to contrast from looks of groups they wish to disassociate with and from there create communities where their products are sold through subscriptions. This is about strategically utilizing the opportunities of today to enhance customer intimacy, anticipate evolving needs, and forge enduring relationships. It is also about moving from selling a beauty product to shaping beauty for a generation. So since it is not technology that is holding any business from doing this, what is it? Would we as leaders rather our competitors define what beauty should be?

This strategic mindset can be applied across diverse sectors. Pension companies, for example, can leverage data to reinforce the sense of security and trust that is paramount to their members, developing personalized retirement planning tools or proactively addressing member concerns through data-driven insights. Mining companies can utilize data to demonstrate transparency and accountability, sharing environmental impact reports and community engagement initiatives with stakeholders. Publications can either simply disseminate stories or become the curator of trusted news in an uncertain world. The former approach might get to achieve the quarterly targets, but it allows others to define the future playing ground.

So as we look at our value propositions, we must make sure it is clear yet not static. Our leadership challenge is not just to identify but also to enable a dynamic learning model that continuously evolves and strengthens our proposition as more users engage with it.

As Minouche Shafik, the president of Columbia University, so aptly put it, "In the past, jobs were about muscles, now they're about brains, but in the future, they'll be about the heart."[4] This reflects a fundamental shift in what is expected from leadership. It's no longer just about skill or intelligence—but about emotional intelligence, trust-building, and the ability to connect deeply with customers, partners, and teams. Companies that grasp the opportunity to combine emotional connections with a constant flow of data can shape products that future-proof themselves. This shift calls for the ability to filter, contextualize, and become the lens, shaping what is seen, prioritized, and acted on, and the decision to determine how the organization's value proposition is best translated into action.

Seeing greater potential builds momentum—once recognized, it shifts what feels possible and raises the bar for what you can achieve. Whether through science, faith, or personal experience, research by psychologist Albert Bandura confirms a powerful truth: Your beliefs about your capabilities are often the key to unlocking your potential.[5] Personal agency plays a defining role in your actual achievements, reinforcing that the ability to envision something greater is not just aspirational; it is consequential.

Visioning is not just about passive optimism; it is a deliberate effort to see higher, look further, and shift what feels possible. It demands stepping away from busyness of daily operations, questioning frames and assumptions, and anticipating market shifts. Placing calculated bets, understanding your role, your data, and your core enables us to shape the future to be attractive to us. A clear ambition does not eliminate uncertainty, but venturing transforms it into forward motion and paves the way for bold movements rather than reactive stumbling. With this comes confidence to shape profit pools as they occur and conviction to shape the conditions to reach further.

Part I Reflections to Motivate Action: Are You Visioning as You Lead in Motion?

Leadership in motion is meeting change with open eyes, expansive breath, and steady hands—moving with clarity, so others feel ready to step forward with you.

- *Ambition as the loudest voice for action:* How strongly does your ambition rise above the noise of daily tasks—offering a direction so clear and energizing that others want to make it theirs too?

- *Clarity on core capability:* Is everyone aligned on the idea that your core capability must be protected and evolved to define your value over time—and if you were an AI, what would you be steering?

- *Anticipating and acting on emerging signals:* How intentionally do you tune in to the signals others miss—and decide whether they are noise or signals of future-defining opportunities?

PART II

....

EXPANDING

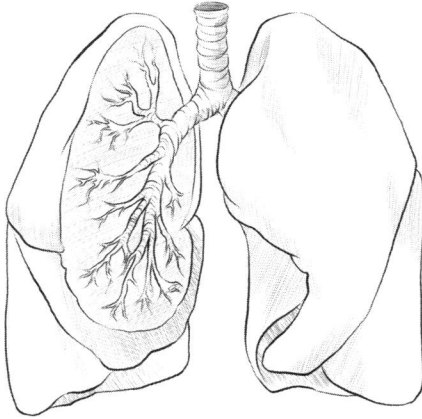

Just as a deep breath fuels endurance, expansive thinking
oxygenates transformation—allowing organizations to
stretch beyond old constraints and accelerate momentum.

4

STANDING ON THE
SHOULDERS OF OTHERS

Just as controlled breathing sustains endurance, broadening your perspective fuels transformation—allowing organizations to expand their reach, push past limitations, and build momentum. Growth thrives on collaboration and external partnerships, combining strengths and extending capabilities. Moreover, true expansion demands a change-resilient approach—one that anticipates shifts in the business landscape and adapts with agility.

Looking at market indices and the performance of the last decade, we see that there has been lots of fluctuation. One area, though, that cannot be neglected is what a major driver of growth the technology sector has been. Where opinions may differ on whether this is the right way to look for future share growth, there are some learnings from within the industry that can be deployed in all sectors and position us well to achieve similar multiples. Beyond innovation and investment, the cloud and AI era leads the way to a new level of collaboration and interdependency built on a product mindset.

A simple example of this approach was seen when in 2023 Google released its upgraded generative AI model, Gemini. While Gemini represented a significant technological leap—for instance, being the first multimodal model—Google recognized that its impact would be maximized if it reached beyond its own Pixel phone devices, which at the time held a relatively modest market share. Instead, Google partnered with Samsung by putting Gemini first in their phones and thereby accessed a vastly wider global smartphone market. Google ensured that Gemini's advanced capabilities would have far greater market penetration, and thereby also broader usage, and Samsung enhanced its product line with the latest AI capabilities without having to develop it themselves. Both for users and for the two companies, this became a win-win solution that prioritized adoption and reach over exclusivity. Latest signals also show that Apple is including Gemini in its beta release of their latest updates, again enabling the technology to reach further and showing the power of platform growth versus brand protection.[1]

It would not have raised a brow if a CEO had chosen to keep the technology to themself with the aim that it could boost sales of Google's devices. However, the strategic choice made reflects a clear, nonemotional product mindset, one that prioritizes scale over ownership. A true product mindset is not about control; it prioritizes impact over ownership and recognizes that leveraging partnerships can accelerate growth, expanding reach and unlocking new opportunities that would not have been possible before.

This type of product mindset is closely aligned with an engineering and building approach. Much like constructing a physical structure, it involves systematically decomposing problems, analyzing available resources, and strategically deciding what to build versus where to leverage existing solutions. An engineer doesn't invest time and resources in crafting every bolt or piece. Instead, they source the best available materials and focus on innovating how those components come together. They may create bespoke parts to add differentiation, but the bulk of the work is in the design, integration, and optimization of existing elements.

In Google's case, integrating Gemini with Samsung's ecosystem was an engineering and business decision to optimize impact and scalability. Evaluating what the market already has to offer, concentrating on what one can uniquely contribute, and prioritizing value over control is an expansive approach to growth. It's a mindset rooted in an understanding of where the organization creates the most value and strategically leverages others to complement its strengths.

This collaborative model is pervasive but not unique to tech, where even fierce competitors join forces to bolster mutual strengths and accelerate their growth. While Apple and Samsung also compete to sell smartphone devices, they still rely on each other for key components. Apple sources OLED screens and used to get their processors from Samsung. This collaboration has helped both companies maintain their respective leadership positions: Apple in user experience and Samsung in advanced component manufacturing. Over time, it has fueled growth for both, allowing them to focus on their core competencies while benefiting from each other's expertise. Partnering strategically rather than competing on every front often leads to amplifying both companies' growth and innovation.

Or what about Amazon Web Services (AWS) cloud platform powering Netflix, enabling scaling content delivery globally while avoiding fixed infrastructure costs? Or Spotify and Uber's integration, where Spotify users can control their music within the Uber app, relying on prebuilt APIs for core location functionalities? This integration enriches the user experience, and Uber benefits from enhanced rider

Partnering strategically rather than competing on every front often leads to amplifying both companies' growth and innovation.

satisfaction, while Spotify gains additional exposure among Uber's user base. Similarly, Google Maps' technology powers Uber's navigation and gains valuable real-time data, reinforcing its position as the default navigation tool in the ride-sharing industry. Each company benefits from the shared ecosystem, using combined data insights and user interaction to refine their own offerings. The lists here could be much longer, and most collaborations will never be seen, but they exist and result in higher engagement and expanded reach across multiple tech-enabled businesses. While many traditional businesses also partner and support each other's growth, the practice of continuously learning from how your components are used across different platforms is far more embedded in tech-enabled ecosystems. This ability to refine and expand offerings through real-time insights likely contributes to the faster growth trajectories seen in digital-first companies.

Leaning into ecosystems this way may for some incumbents seem easy to say no to, as holding back progress may let businesses cling to their current positions longer. However, the world does not stand still, and the only thing you are, in fact, saying no to is your own participation in the success. Looking at the momentum around and selectively, strategically, and wisely partnering for noncore elements is what generates the fuel to join the fastest growth.

Viewing expansion and growth as part of a larger ecosystem offers businesses a path to wider, scalable success—where shared platforms, and open collaboration, combined with strategic clarity, can create an adaptable, forward-looking business model. Leveraging a focused product mindset also helps organizations optimize resources and gain operational efficiency by helping identify overreliance, uncovering alternatives, and therefore enabling greater resilience and agility. At the same time, a clear mutual interdependence within an open platform gives space for focused innovation and for aligning resources where they can have the greatest impact.

POSSIBILITIES OFTEN OUTPACE
LEADERSHIP READINESS

By far, the world's most used navigation system is Google Maps. The route optimization algorithm behind this was originally built by Google's own operations research team in response to the task of mapping the best way to efficiently cover the surface of the world's streets for Google Street View cars. For this, they built optimization AIs to plan, schedule, and execute routes. Some years later, the city of Toronto approached Google and asked whether it could help understand what the optimal placement of bus stops in the city was. The same team extended their models with traffic patterns, people movements, and so on. Some years later, again, a leading global delivery company with 20 million or more daily deliveries also approached the Google team for help, and they added capabilities for the AI to handle constraints such as delivery slots, driver schedule limitations, traffic, rerouting options in case of breakdowns, and so on. The capability built was now so powerful that it enabled the delivery company to execute their full operations with an impressive 25 percent smaller fleet and naturally corresponding massive fuel reductions.

Today, this is both a consumer product that continuously evolves and an AI that businesses can integrate into their own operations. Integrating this AI is extending your capacity with all the learnings built by the Google engineers over decades and is hugely powerful. If you, for instance, want to combine a demand forecasting AI with an AI that tells you where to best place delivery partners to meet that demand, these pretrained AIs enable you to solely bring data and leverage others' optimization recommendation. Building that yourself would take immense effort to do. It is a win-win, because in this instance, traffic is relatively subjective, and we are therefore happy to leverage the expertise of others, to stand on their shoulders. But who should we as leaders trust to train other models?

I occasionally teach executives at Copenhagen Business School, where I also serve on the board, and there we often do an exercise. I ask them whether they use Google Maps. Generally all say yes, some directly from its own app, some from Apple CarPlay, and some from in-vehicle integrated Google Maps navigation—but fundamentally all rely on Google Maps underneath. I ask them about other AIs, such as vision AI. Would they trust that Google has looked at so many pictures that when it says it is a dog, it is a dog? Or what about when it looks at an X-ray—is Google right to determine what is seen? What about when we combine the two capabilities? Given that Google has vision AI in cars alongside Google Maps navigation (and more), it can be assumed that no other company has had access to as much data to train models on this. Does this then mean that Google should own self-driving cars? Or would you be more comfortable if that was Ford, SAIC, Mercedes, Geely, or Tesla? And should they do it with Google's technology or build their own?

Today, technology is developing at such a pace that the capabilities and training far outpace that of the industries that would typically be bringing many of these services. This currently creates a gap in the market as tech companies often remain in their product realm, whereas operational companies seek to use technology that has been made relevant for them. Many businesses today still spend a fortune with system integrators where products are connected specifically for the business, giving very little scalability and acceleration for the business or industry. This may be seen as standing on the shoulders of each other, but it is done in a linear rather than exponential way.

I have often been asked by customers, "Can't Google just go into building supply-chain-specific optimization models for automotive? Or combine raw material pricing with consumer interest, to steer production of EV batteries to where it would have the greatest CO_2 impact for the world?" And so on. But Google does not currently hold the industry-specific knowledge to do so and enjoys much wider growth from having technology that is applicable to a wider audience. But maybe you do?

This is where partnerships across tech and industries become critical. A platform model—a powerful concept that goes beyond ownership to prioritize openness and interconnectedness—can unlock great opportunities. One example of a traditional-plus-tech collaboration is John Deere's activities in support of precision agriculture. John Deere, a leader in agricultural machinery, has integrated AI technology into its farming equipment to provide real-time data analysis on crop conditions. This helps farmers optimize planting, watering, and harvesting through data-driven decisions, boosting yields and efficiency. John Deere offers higher-value solutions, enhancing margins and market position, while their tech and edge-computing partner expands into agriculture, unlocking new revenue streams. Such partnerships create competitive advantages and diversify growth. While John Deere currently does not sell its precision agriculture technology to other players in the industry, they do hold an extensive ecosystem where their customers continuously train their models, reinforcing and strengthening their position and distancing themselves from the market with their customers.

These models play to open markets, where collaboration and external partnerships often drive growth. In certain parts of the world especially, we have also seen companies successfully take control of the entire value chain. This approach typically makes them more resilient to external pressures, not from optionality but from control, as well as gives power to influence markets in preferential ways. However, this level of autonomy comes with a significant requirement: confidence that the organization holds enough intrinsic value to shape its own future. It demands access to substantial investment and the ability to leverage data effectively to stay ahead of the curve—conditions that remain out of reach for most companies. And importantly, it requires a change-resilient strategic direction where one assumes all developments can be predicted within the business.

This is also why despite many smaller businesses trying to fill the gap and connect technology with industries, there is often inadequate access to data to connect themselves in a meaningful way to larger ecosystems that would allow their solutions to mature. Without access to sufficient data, their ability to train and improve their products and drive industry-wide transformation remains limited. Established players such as GE, Bosch, and Siemens have long recognized this opportunity and are actively making these moves. However, for many industries, this missing layer still remains. No leaders have stepped up to it.

Let's revisit Groupe Renault and their ability to make fast non-emotional assessments of the market's needs and acknowledge where partnerships would accelerate them. They built multiple partnerships to ensure expansive transformation. Just as with Google, the partnerships spanned from manufacturing and the ability to digitally understand the production, to marketing and go-to-market strategy, to supply chains, the configurations of cars, and software-defined vehicles. Through this collaboration, Renault has not only streamlined its processes but also positioned itself as a tech-enabled leader in the automotive industry. This demonstrates how traditional sectors can leverage digital partnerships to drive efficiency and competitive advantage—enabling them to leapfrog many larger players in the industry.

PROGRESS OVER QUICK WINS

This form of expansive collaborative thinking has been at the heart of research-heavy tech businesses for decades. A great illustration of this is a research paper openly published by teams at Google in 2017, titled "Attention Is All You Need."[2] This paper introduced the transformer architecture, which has since revolutionized natural language processing and AI. Its impact has led to the creation of numerous AI models, forming the foundation for companies such as OpenAI, Anthropic, Mistral AI, Cohere, and Hugging Face. Major tech companies including Meta, Microsoft, Amazon, Apple, and, of course, Google have also heavily benefited from this. According to ChatGPT, this makes the conservative value of "Attention Is All You Need" in the range of $5–10 trillion over the next decade. Whether this number is right or not is less important than the fact that a market was created through progressive thinking and exposing this to the world, and the ripple effect of innovation underscores the profound impact and long-term benefits of shared knowledge and contributions to a collaborative research ecosystem.

This is not a unique case. When the Human Genome Project mapped the entire human genome for the world, it was estimated to have generated nearly $1 trillion in value.[3] When Sir Tim Berners-Lee revolutionized information sharing with the World Wide Web, he shared the protocols and encouraged global adoption, something that is now so valuable it is impossible to put a price on. Or, in the realm of more traditional business, Toyota has a history of sharing manufacturing philosophies and production systems, which has helped them maintain their position as leader in this space and contributed to a market cap higher than $300 billion,[4] or in examples such as when Shell and ExxonMobil decided to jointly develop new technologies for exploration, significantly minimizing the cost of research and development and enabling increased revenues.[5]

Today, geopolitical tensions and shareholder expectations often push for absolute wins over relative progress, but the evolution of AI and open research has shown that in platform-driven worlds, the biggest wins unfold over time. Those who pursue transformational impact with a clear strategic approach, not just immediate dominance, are the ones who leave the strongest legacy.

ASSESSING RISK

Naturally, there are many stories of attempts to collaborate and scale that have not taken off. Some because of a lack of differentiated data access, some because of insufficient funding, others because of a lack of willingness to commit, and many because of the lack of willingness of partners to lean in. For instance, when IBM launched its blockchain technology, there were high expectations of it revolutionizing several industries—banking and supply chains, just to mention a few. However, the exact premise of blockchain, removing a central validating authority, was in fact the fear that held many back. The hesitation was not just about trust but also about supporting something that could eventually commoditize their own role in the value chain.

But it is not about technology, and blockchain is certainly not the answer to all the questions it has been linked to over time. However, I embrace the principle of being open to evolving my proposition to become a part of a bigger ecosystem. Placing myself in an ecosystem that grows my business with and for me is an opportunity much more used in the technology world today—and the market capitalizations of these businesses clearly show the value.

Naturally, partnering is a matter of trust, and like in interactions between human relations, clarity of intent and honesty about what complementary skills you can offer each other is critical. In my experience, having fronted several transformation partnerships, there is no doubt that your track record and reputation also open many doors. An area that is often neglected is the openness and honesty of articulating what is known versus what is believed, as well as being aware of each other's incentives. I am still surprised by how rarely clear expectations on gains become an open conversation. When done right, it creates clarity and comfort and enables the other party to make a decision on stronger grounds.

> Managing ecosystems is about constructing dynamic, flexible systems that allow others to plug in and contribute without diluting your own essence.

This is not about one big strategic decision but about an ongoing curiosity of what and who moves in the market and a view of how we as leaders can deploy ourselves effectively in a continuously morphing ecosystem. It requires agility and a strong awareness of your decomposed business to see what around it could be complementary and accelerating. Managing ecosystems is about constructing dynamic, flexible systems that allow others to plug in and contribute without diluting your own essence.

Would business decisions, for instance, look different if you turned your external attention toward movements in your ecosystem and what research is enabling, to consider how you could best connect services to serve your customers? Or are you confined by what you control? Are you constantly validating whether your strategy leverages the best thinking on offer at the current time?

Blending a clear vision with a practical, honest assessment of what is available, the value, and what can be built through partnerships is key in leadership. It is about fostering a mindset in which collaboration is valued more highly than control, and in which trust in the right partnerships fuels growth in ways that would be impossible on our own. Leaders who are able to navigate market shifts with agility, leverage insights from diverse sources, and from there make informed decisions to drive the business forward will take the lead. Playing into open, adaptable ecosystems is essential, as they provide the foundation for collaboration and more targeted innovation through a greater value of ideas, enabling businesses to scale via external collaborators. If you understand the power of these ecosystems, you will expand your reach, drive sustained impact, and foster long-term success by continuously evolving through collective intelligence and shared resources.

5

COLLECTIVE INTELLIGENCE
FOR GENERATIVE CONVERSATIONS

Expansion through external partnerships is a powerful move for shaping the future, but so is the ability to capture a team's collective intelligence. At the core of achieving more is expansive thinking—the ability to create space for growth. For me, one of the most rewarding experiences is engaging in a generative conversation where both participants arrive at insights and conclusions we couldn't have reached alone. These moments foster new connections, spark the exchange of ideas, and expand collective understanding. It is in these moments that I feel the deepest appreciation for human engagement—where complementary perspectives push the boundaries of what is possible.

Beyond the individual benefits, generative conversations activate powerful group dynamics. They trigger positive emotions, social bonding, and collaboration. In fact, research shows that meaningful social interactions activate the brain's reward system in ways similar to food and pleasure.[1] From a mental performance standpoint, generative conversations naturally allow teams to think together instead of individually, reducing weight and complexity on the individual and creating a sense of challenges being more possible to overcome.[2]

For businesses, this is not just about better conversations—it is about better outcomes. Studies on collective intelligence show that teams engaging in diverse, open discussions consistently outperform individuals and homogenous groups in creativity, decision-making, and problem-solving.[3] Generative conversations not only drive innovation but also increase engagement, motivation, and smarter decision-making across the organization. Leaders who embody curiosity foster cultures of adaptability, innovation, and accountability. Curiosity becomes the foundation for resilience, trust, and transformative progress.

All leaders have hopefully felt the difference between engaged teams and those who move only to complete a task they have been given. In fact, according to Gallup research in 2023, companies with a highly engaged workforce have shown to outperform their peers by 147 percent in earnings per share.[4] Creating an environment where employees feel empowered, valued, and recognized for their contributions—while also seeing growth opportunities for themselves and for the business—drives engagement.

Clear expectations are often cited as drivers of successful engagement. However, they only lead to meaningful impact when tied to a clear sense of purpose or ambition. The common mistake is assuming that clarity alone is enough, when in fact overfocusing on expectations without connecting them to a larger ambition limits contribution. If you instead set a clear and ambitious goal and empower teams to meaningfully contribute to it, you will both leverage resources most effectively and reach higher.

Naturally, leadership plays a critical role in creating an environment where collective intelligence can thrive. While many leaders claim they support this, the reality is that behavior, incentive structures, and systems often reinforce silos. This disconnect between rhetoric and reality hinders progress and blocks the potential of their human capital. Businesses must foster a culture of knowledge-sharing, collaboration, and continuous learning. This is critical for innovative thinking, but it is just as essential for avoiding premature alignment that may overlook critical risks or opportunities.

This reflection can be about people or about tech architecture. Organizational structures and hierarchies of the past could be seen as legacy systems, frameworks that hold and protect the status quo. Meanwhile, interoperable, cloud-based data platforms with AI capabilities can enable learning from data across processes. But changing one without the other will not deliver the desired value, so if a business has made tech purchases but forgotten to upgrade the leadership approach to enable the organization, value will falter. Or it will become like the many businesses that have spent the last decade building data lakes, massive pools of information that remain inaccessible because they are structured based on outdated siloes—lacking clear tagging, governance, or integration. Technology alone does not create intelligence. Without enabling the organization to discover, query, extract, innovate, and redesign, technology investments become like giving a hungry person a fish instead of *teaching* them to fish. Any potential value will be short-lived.

> Without enabling the organization to discover, query, extract, innovate, and redesign, technology investments become like giving a hungry person a fish instead of *teaching* them to fish.

While there is no blame intended in this, many businesses operate this way as a natural result of growth, scaling, and a human fear of losing control. But today's technology, particularly AI, demands that leaders reconsider whether they are missing opportunities by not leveraging their organization's collective intelligence more effectively.

ENABLING COLLECTIVE INTELLIGENCE WITH DATA

During my time at Diageo before the AI wave, I was part of a team looking at data correlations to best optimize the advertising and promotion spend. We combined years of store sell-out data, consumer sentiment data, media spend, and impressions, as well as weather data by brand and geography. We confirmed our hypothesis that some brands were so responsive that when it rained in one country, shifting money to TV there would give a higher uplift than any other brand or country could deliver. Or seeing that for some categories, if sentiment was low, no amount of promotion could shift sales. It was just math. The challenge was not doing the data correlations or the predictions; the challenge was the conversation with the country managers when our suggested optimizations affected their chance of hitting previously set targets, against which they had staffed their business. What started as a marketing exercise turned into a temperature check of how connected and ready we were to optimize the business's bottom line and how committed the organization was to the larger ambition of profitable growth.

Just like combining these different data points suggested here, there was huge value in harnessing the power of *different* minds, *different* experiences, and *different* ways of seeing the world. In this way, we could, in fact, get to a more predictable outcome and better ROI of our spend. It is just a simple illustration highlighting that leaders who try to cling to fixed dashboards mistaking them for power are setting themselves up for irrelevance in a world where the ability to synthesize diverse perspectives and adapt rapidly is the true differentiator. As AI accelerates the flow of knowledge, the role of IQ is shifting, and the strongest leaders are not just those who are able to consume information but those who connect, question, and enhance it. AI may surface information, but human curiosity still determines how it is applied.

I also had the pleasure of working in close partnership with the team at one of the world's largest airline groups as they were deploying a state-of-the-art operational solver for one of their airlines. Airline operations are one of the most complex optimization challenges one can find. There are millions of considerations and often conflicting interests, whether you ask crew teams, aircraft rotation teams, passenger teams, or ground control. One can optimize for lowest fuel consumption, for customer satisfaction, for efficient ground handling, and so on. There are so many potentially divergent interests.

What the team did was first make sure that all the data from each function was accessible. They then ran separate processes to document decisions from each function, both physically and through machine learning. This all served as input—not as the answer. Next, the business parameters or rules were set—for example, physical constraints, legal requirements, and seating requirements. All of this was then fed into a grand solver, which weighed the different constraints and optimized for the best outcome. It is not uncommon in business, as in this instance, that there is not one right answer; it often depends on the objective at the time and the subjective lens or data view. A decision that is right for some may be suboptimal for others—for example, the cheapest operations could have a cost on customer experience. What Google did with the airline was to allow many solvers to run in parallel. Some solvers were fast and gave a quick suggestion for a decent answer for all parameters, others looked into more niche data sets and took a longer time to recommend an outcome, and still others did something in between. And then again, these were compared for the best outcome. By not pre-deciding which method was the strongest for this complex question, the teams felt important and appreciated, since all contributions were being evaluated. The volume of data considered in this type of optimization remains huge and complex, but the AI solver gave the operations teams a decision-support tool, enabling them to now have one of the most profitable operations in the world. The airline group is, at the current time, rolling it across their wider group and several competitors are asking whether they can partner or purchase the service even from their competitor, simply as the quality would justify it.

None of these teams could have done this on their own; nor would any human brain have had the intelligence to balance these parameters. Equally important, the approach with which it is built means that for every flight the solver looks at, it gets wiser. The business, therefore, is taking its collective intelligence and every day surely distancing itself from its competitors.

As a part of this partnership, I also had the pleasure of spending time with all the operational leaders of the airline group. Even with the backdrop of the massive success and unanimous backing of the operations solver, I again experienced the gap between rational support and emotional buy-in. At a large-scale meeting, I fell into dialogue with some of the pilots; the individuals whom we all frequently trust with our lives to get us safely in the air and back on the ground again. We got talking about the potential of connecting data points for better decision-making and what this would mean for them. They seemed to not follow my line of questioning. They were the captains. Their job was to know it all, to be in charge—not to have some machine on the ground advise them. That would go against everything they believed in. I then flipped it and asked them whether there was anything they wished they knew that they didn't know. Silence. But when prompted from the room with ideas—such as a shortage of bridges at the destination, causing delays to park; whether de-icing capacity was under pressure at the connecting airport; or whether an incoming group of passengers had a loyalty status that meant one had to wait for them—one of the pilots started to see that this was helpful. The point was, of course, not to expose them or point out that no one is an oracle but to highlight the number of influences that could affect their decisions, which they ordinarily had no way of seeing.

Even strong performers can still often be suboptimizing their potential simply because of a lack of sight of critical facts. While we as leaders cannot and should not uncover all the missing connections, it is our role to foster a culture of collective intelligence: a wider base of knowledge to learn from and a continued responsibility to expand both human and AI learning.

SHAPING A CULTURE FOR PSYCHOLOGICALLY SAFE RELATIONSHIPS

Knowledge sharing is a deeply human act, requiring trust, vulnerability, and a willingness to engage with others' perspectives. Experience shows that this is best built by small moments, of consistent behaviors that signal reliability, authenticity, and mutual respect in information sharing. The reality is, though, that in many organizations, hierarchies have been built out of knowledge as power, and as leaders we rarely are conscious of how quickly learning can be inhibited by our own weight in conversations. But when creating environments where knowledge-sharing becomes a collective norm rather than an individual risk, organizations move from isolated intelligence to collaborative environments where employees feel seen and heard and where employees feel empowered to explore new ideas and challenge the status quo.

All this rests on the bedrock of psychological safety, creating a space for free knowledge sharing to flourish and for teams to challenge ideas without fear. It has been seen that psychological safety can outperform skills multiple times. For that simple reason, it is one of the most accessible ways to access an individual's full potential.

In environments lacking psychological safety, the brain defaults to survival mode, diverting energy from problem-solving to active engagement in self-preservation. Creating the same, and as real a reaction as if it had been in physical danger, the brain will protect information, reduce collaboration, develop a sense of increased anxiety, and exhibit higher risk aversion—not because they decide to, but as a neurological consequence. In essence, psychological safety is not a soft skill; it's the hard currency of high-performance teams, one that gives space for expansive thinking, fuels endurance, and oxygenates transformation.

LEADING GENERATIVE CONVERSATIONS

I have unfortunately also encountered misunderstood attempts at this. Organizations signal support to grow and offer an inordinate amount of training, but without tying these efforts to any ambition. While access to knowledge is great, it does *not* automatically translate to collective intelligence.

I worked closely with an impressive business across several waves of engagement. Their business had always been open to trying and testing new things, and they had made the investment to connect hundreds of systems together. A top executive knew that he also had talented teams with lots of expertise across the globe who all had the passion to contribute to reach further. However at one point, as we were doing a workshop in that room, he realized: The very culture that had given him the richness of input was now the challenge for him to connect and scale it. The positive, collaborative culture had also led to a misunderstood encouragement, which made teams accountable for bringing pieces to the table. Yet no one felt the accountability for combining these into the larger shifts. Openness without direction and a willingness to build on each other's thinking just becomes a misunderstood form of consensus.

Openness is not saying yes to everything, it is about being curious about everything and finding what adds value—which is then given purpose and role. What is not deemed valuable must respectfully lead to clear messaging and refocused attention. As the executive reflected on this challenge, it became clear that it was the absence of a unifying ambition and accountability toward this that was missing. Without it, even well-intended activities and innovation risk becoming a distraction rather than progress.

In fact, some of the world's largest companies struggle with this. Leaders in consumer products, home furniture, and tech face similar challenges—misunderstood empowerment. Innovation, sometimes clouded by politeness, has led to behaviors in which initiatives are started all over. They may be good or bad, but the challenge is that there is no culture and behavior to scale them; instead, they become a resource drain and misuse of modern leadership.

Furthermore, too many decisions are being made without scrutiny of the quality or source of the data. The risk of making choices based on outdated assumptions, biased perspectives (confirmation bias), or even misinformation is only growing, and the need to challenge not only the data itself but also who is producing it, why it exists, and what may be missing remains. This is why respectful critical thinking, cross-checking sources, open-minded testing, and contextualizing data remains important. More and more, we see that the real differentiator is not simply access but discernment.

In modern leadership, the balance between autonomy and alignment remains critical. As leaders, I believe we need to role model being curious yet discerning—asking deeper questions, testing ideas, and thinking critically about the information we encounter. True collective intelligence doesn't emerge from endless experimentation or scattered initiatives; it comes from intentional efforts—where inquisitive exploration and curiosity fuels progress, learning ties back to meaningful ambitions, and contributions coalesce into something stronger than their individual parts. This creates teams that don't just absorb knowledge but actively apply it to solve real problems and move beyond simply being "trained" individuals to becoming a dynamic force of collective intelligence that drives meaningful results.

We see this kind of applied learning most clearly in early development. Children do not learn by passively receiving instructions—they experiment, adjust when something does not work, and build on each other's ideas. They are motivated not just by outcomes but by the process of shared creation. In business, it is no different. When change is treated as a static plan, engagement remains surface-level. But when people can shape it, interact with it, and see their own imprint in the outcome, participation deepens. The companies that navigate transformation well do not depend on isolated brilliance—they create conditions where progress compounds, where people connect, adapt, and elevate each other's contributions. That is when collective intelligence becomes a real force.

6

MOBILIZING EXPANSIVE THINKING

Being open is essential for learning. However, being open to expanding knowledge is hard work. You need to challenge everything, as it is built to reinforce what you already know. My cupboard is filled with stylish, crafted, elegant designer cups. There are two espresso cups that stand out. I love these two because I bought them with my sons on vacation in Greece. One has a handwritten quote from Socrates on the side: "Wisdom begins with wonder."

Tapping into a sense of wonder may feel like the opposite of a world where algorithms predict what I want and serve it to me. A lunch menu in the local kitchen, likely selected based on what I will like; the song Spotify suggests; and the answers Google or ChatGPT serve me are all built to continue the path I am on, not to challenge it.

Openness demands you do more than resist assumptions—it requires that you actively seek alternative perspectives. In organizations, this means working beyond default patterns, using complementary data models to surface blind spots, and deliberately uncovering insights that would otherwise remain hidden. Left unchecked, decisions will be shaped by what is easy to access rather than what is necessary to understand. The real effort lies in ensuring that learning isn't just a passive process but an intentional investment—one that expands, rather than narrows, the way forward. And one where everyone understands that the power of building on each other's thinking is not just about innovation; it's also about return on investment.

Think about it: Why are the most powerful coaching questions also open-ended questions? Can you tell me more? What else could be true? It is anchoring where you are while inviting you to move further. Build a new hypothesis. Leaders may have been trained to be conclusive and create clarity, but as they ask "why" and "what if" instead of accepting surface-level explanations, curiosity—especially intellectual curiosity—becomes a powerful tool for building a habit of openness. The time spent on learning ranges widely depending on sources; however, 5 to 20 percent of the time is not rare. I have personally found that the time spent on learning at the executive level exceeds the time taken by middle management, increasing the natural tendency of focus on daily tasks at this level. This tendency risks creating a bottleneck in knowledge flow and hinders organizational agility. When leaders genuinely demonstrate curiosity at all levels, it becomes contagious, fostering a culture in which continuous improvement and learning are valued. This means that not only will individuals grow, but teams will also continuously raise the bar and carry wider responsibility to venture higher and greater.

Years ago, I came across a slide; its source is long forgotten, but its impact has stayed with me. It showed an iceberg. At the top, just above the waterline, were the executives, with "4%" written next to them—4 percent knowledge on a given topic. Just below, the direct reports of the executives, these leaders showed 9 percent, followed by managers at 74 percent, and at the base, the lowest level of the organization, showing they hold 100 percent of the knowledge needed on a certain topic. The exact percentages may not be precise for every organization, but directionally, they hold up. As executives, our expertise must encompass so many topics that having 4 percent on any one of them is probably about right. Yet decisions are often escalated to levels where detailed knowledge is limited.

This is why I believe executive leadership is largely about setting the right context—so that the most relevant 4 percent is surfaced at the right time. Each layer needs to understand the ambition, the broader context, and with that, pass on not just information but the *right* information. Only with openness can we determine which parts of the 100 percent should move up to the 74 percent, where interdependencies come into play; to the 9 percent, where resource allocations often must align; and finally, to the 4 percent, where it needs to land as a clear contribution to a shared ambition. If done well, this isn't a game of telephone, in which the message is distorted from one repetition to the next, but a structured way to ensure that what truly matters makes it to the right level.

This slide is also a healthy reminder for those fully immersed in their 100 percent, who sometimes lack context and therefore forget that they are an important yet small piece of a much bigger puzzle. This expertise sits beneath the surface, and without openness—both from above and from below—critical knowledge risks staying hidden. When those at the top don't create space to select the right input, or when those at the base don't see how their knowledge connects to the broader ambition, organizations risk making decisions in an echo chamber.[1]

But this isn't just an organizational and growth challenge—it reflects how people learn and process information in general. Many businesses try to support sharing through activities such as lunch and learns, casual gatherings where colleagues can share with each other, or through executives traveling around the world to spend a day in the life of (DILO) their teams or customers. These are all well-intended activities; however, there is a fundamental challenge: These exercises are designed for exposure rather than transformation. They often become either pure inspiration or, worse, environments where a subordinate's performance is inadvertently being assessed. The pressure of such a moment rarely enables mutual learning.

Jeff Bezos famously asked his teams to start any project with a press release describing what it would become once live in the market. This approach represents a strong shift from asking for a fact exchanges to instead seeking an applied understanding and forcing teams out of their own frame of reference to consider how something would take shape in the real world.

True growth and understanding go beyond recognizing familiar patterns; it requires seeing the world from perspectives fundamentally different from your own. The brain is wired to seek similarity and, once we find a connection, we often assume the rest aligns with what we already know. But this limits real comprehension. When learning is tied to a shared ambition—rather than passive exposure—it becomes transformational, not just informational. Understanding isn't about mapping everything back to our own frame of reference; it's about seeing ideas as they exist in their own context. As Julian Baggini explores in *How the World Thinks*, true openness means engaging with different viewpoints on their terms, not just fitting them into existing structures.[2]

> When learning is tied to a shared ambition—rather than passive exposure—it becomes transformational, not just informational.

Openness in decision-making isn't just about surfacing the right insights—it's about creating the conditions for people to act on them. Without that, even the best strategies risk being built on incomplete understanding. The same tendency that makes individuals default to familiar thinking plays out at scale in organizations. If there is no space for what sits beneath the surface, decisions end up being driven by what is easiest to recognize rather than what is most relevant.

THE RUSH TO BE RIGHT

Today, businesses are rushing into AI investments—and they should be. Unfortunately, this approach doesn't always manifest in the way that will drive the biggest impact. This is something I've seen time and again when leading strategic business transformation at Google. The initial focus is often on technology and data, but the real challenge is how the organization engages with it.

A tool I've used often illustrates transformation through the different stages of a butterfly. At the base, it shows a data platform—not a single monolith of answers but a foundation that connects information and enables exploration. Next, evolution of the butterfly is data access culture—the collective behaviors that make it okay to access data across silos, ask questions of others, create hypotheses, and uncover new patterns without repercussions for looking beyond your own space. This step often dominates discussions. Because without a true data access culture, the final two stages—AI, to uncover patterns and extract hidden insights, and acceleration, to play into the ecosystem and scale—become irrelevant. Many companies cut themselves off from these higher-value steps simply because they haven't created the openness required to get there.[3]

This cannot be solved through investment, drive, or strong tech. If talent can't access the right information, decision-making becomes guesswork. Imagine training sophisticated AI models on narrow, siloed datasets—that is state-of-the-art technology with a blindfold on. It is like businesses pouring resources into marketing campaigns, only to discover their product is out of stock. You can spend your time chasing disconnected KPIs, or you can build a data access culture that empowers teams to see and solve problems. Given the right information and the freedom to act on it, they will uncover far more than any one leader ever could alone. People don't make the wrong decisions intentionally; they make them because they just don't have the data to see otherwise.

> People don't make the wrong decisions intentionally; they make them because they just don't have the data to see otherwise.

To nudge such a change, consider whether you should have some of your teams swap KPIs. The engrained and cultural tie to their old remit is likely to still exist within for a while but measuring them on someone else's objectives will certainly make them consider things differently. The ability to challenge assumptions, recognize blind spots, and see beyond immediate constraints isn't just useful in data strategy; it's essential in any high-stakes environment.

Having worked in companies with a broad geographical footprint and with global businesses, I have always been conscious of challenging biases. I did this, on its simplest level, in my early years of gathering insights by visiting foreign families in Brazil or Vietnam to understand their consumption patterns, which far challenged what we had assumed in an office in London, and, later, when I looked at how US East Coast and West Coast, Swiss, and French business schools read the current business world differently and teach leadership in slightly different ways. We are all biased, but we need to be aware of this and act with the awareness of this. Only when we are able to recognize these frames of reference are we able to understand the nuances, the small data that might be exactly what can accelerate you—if you don't rush past first.

I was at a board seminar at a leading business university outside Paris, the Institut Européen d'Administration des Affaires (INSEAD). When the discussion turned to how confidence influences decision-making, the professor posed a question: "Which team would you pick for an important assignment? Team A is 80 percent skilled and 80 percent confident. Team B is 60 percent skilled and 40 percent confident." There was no alignment on the answer in the room, but interestingly, most felt very confident in their own choice of team. The majority of people selected the team that was badged as 80 percent skilled.

Reality is, though, that the degree level of confidence is a massive risk, as this confidence will fool them into expecting they know the answer, whereas those who are aware they are still learning will proceed with curiosity and respect for what they need to learn. The business results the professor shared with us afterward clearly showed that the teams identified as highly confident and highly skilled had been beaten by competition, whereas all of the businesses observed that resembled the more immature skill set without overconfidence had exceeded market growth. They were simply supported by the right attitude.

Some may call it intellectual curiosity, but it is also a matter of being strategic. Openness isn't just about absorbing different perspectives—it's about using them to see what others might miss. Being open to new angles is a powerful way to uncover connections that haven't yet been made—the kind that shifts thinking and drives competitive advantage. The same principle is visible in nature. The most resilient ecosystems are the most diverse. They thrive not because of a single dominant force but because of functional overlaps, adaptability, and strong interdependencies that reduce risk. Survival has never been about being the strongest—it has always been about being able to adapt. This principle holds true in organizations, industries, and leadership itself.

ENABLING OPENNESS

Openness has proven to be crucial for growth, requiring you to actively challenge biases to expand your ambitions. The next step is turning that openness into momentum—embedding it within the organization to drive real progress.

I was once part of a commercial leadership team, which our well-respected leader, with pride and excitement, called the "social experiment." He held a lot of clout in the business and had a long-standing positive trajectory. He had been a company man through and through and had earned the right in this very traditional business to rattle the cages a bit, so where others would have been questioned, he was not. The team he put together had 50-50 gender split, three very different demographic backgrounds, but an even wider range of ways of thinking. There was the process-by-the-book person, the diligent-sharp type, the engaging sales leader, the maverick, and then me. In hindsight, we were not even that diverse a group after all, just on relative terms to the rest of the organization. We all enjoyed each other's company and had good respect for one another, but every debate took us days. The leader had acknowledged the need for diversity in thinking and styles and was willing to create the space for us to learn together. It was hard, but important. I am convinced we all had our moments of swearing about the process and lack of common ground, but we had the shared goal and therefore we kept at it. It did work, at least mostly. We managed to move mountains. It did create results, and we did manage to create bonds and have memorable laughs together. We showed the organization that we were investing in making this work.

The experiment started to crumble when hub-and-spoke conversations with our leader grew. Individually, we went to our boss to have debates and align with him and walked out of the office with gratitude and triumph because we felt we had achieved a win. We had not. Instead, we were getting back to siloes and not taking responsibility for delivering together. Our drive for individual progress was overtaking the collective momentum.

I have since observed many customers leadership teams, and I often see this pattern repeat. There are good intentions on shared ambition, but you can quickly recognize where people break out and lead with their own points most in the quest to shine. I have also many times since reflected on whether I have inadvertently encouraged my own team members by meeting them in their individual motivations, instead of helping them make their views clearer for others. Have I always been willing to go slow to go faster? And I wonder—have you?

Beyond the deeper reflections on leadership, I am often asked by fellow leaders, "What can I tangibly do for my business today to reap the benefits of technology innovations such as AI?" The reality is that often the best thing that can be done is to clearly remind of the ambition, give access and space to explore, and actively get out of their way. Clear half a day of their schedules every two weeks for a period and let them use exploration tools such as generative AI on own data sets (e.g., Notebook LM). Create excitement and reward the findings.

If you challenge your teams to venture and come up with innovative contributions, and frame them appropriately, you will find they most likely already have a lot of bottled thinking within them. Bring them together in new constellations—such as bringing procurement in with front-line sales? Or IT infrastructure with the facility teams? Let them connect with people on the same level from other functions rather than having more layers in one room.

The best thing we as leaders can do personally is to stop limiting innovation, think about how many barriers are created for free thinking to flow, and actively take ownership of removing them. On practical terms, what do we need to stop doing, stop controlling, stop holding back, and stop blocking things that we do not fully yet comprehend? To look ourselves in the mirror and ask whether we have truly created the environment to be challenged? And to be ready to also see who does not step up to the challenge, and who is not actively positioning themselves as part of the business's future?

Concepts such as mashing—an innovative technique where you combine seemingly unrelated or disparate elements—are great for unlocking new and innovative solutions. Mashing sparks originality, breaks out of conventional thinking, and explores unexpected possibilities. It is much more than a fun gimmick; it is hugely valuable for business. In fact, the smartphone, GPS, Post-it Notes, Velcro, and the Dyson hand dryer all claim to have been invented by this thinking. And if in doubt, be reminded that reaching an ambition beyond the linear path requires expansive thinking.

At Google, defaulting to open is part of the company's DNA. This means that, by design, information is accessible. You can search internal drives and find what others may have created about a topic, you can open it, read it, see the author, ping them a question on chat, and even write comments in their document. Many businesses may claim the same; however, two elements felt very different to me when entering this culture: (1) the extent of the access and (2) that everything was self-serve. I have many times gone to bed at night having finished some thinking and woken up the next day to comments in my document from people I had never met. They were working in spaces adjacent to me and wanted to learn from my thinking, just as I wanted to from theirs. It was incredibly powerful, since I had never known to ask for their point of view, but they added perspectives I could never have come to on my own. And as the owner of the material, it was still my responsibility to understand, assess, and decide how to include (or not) into the thinking. The element of everything being self-serve is, however, wasted if everyone is not aimed at a strong shared ambition—a constantly reminded vision where contributions are shared, so that everyone can reflect on what complementarity they should search for and can contribute to. When it works, it is exponential, and it has an added bonus of training leadership skills to all, as everyone trains the skills of articulating value and targeting efforts.

Naturally, there are exceptions to this, though these are few and far between: selective product briefs, patent papers, the closed investment assessments, and so on, but mobilizing your workforce to effectively contribute to the same goal is one of the fastest ways to turn the saying "people are the biggest resources" into business value in a digitized world.

The more leaders demonstrate that knowledge sharing is integral to the success of the organization, the more employees will feel motivated to participate in this collaborative exchange. Having seen structures such as peer-to-peer bonuses create a great sense of trust and responsibility and, interestingly, even though one can easily fear the impact and generosity, budgets in fact rarely get spent in full. The potential and sentiment are worth significantly more than the cost.

HOW DATA ARCHITECTURES LAYER WITH ORGANIZATIONAL INSIGHTS

A leader's ability to create space for exploration and discussion shapes how their organization operates, how decisions are made, and ultimately, how adaptable it becomes. The way a company structures its data, the insights it prioritizes, and the assumptions it challenges all reflect its leadership mindset.

No business can be open if its leaders are not. Some of the most forward-thinking companies have turned this into an advantage, not by having all the answers upfront but by creating environments where the best answers emerge. Patagonia has built an unshakeable reputation by openly acknowledging both its achievements and its setbacks in sustainability efforts, reinforcing deep trust among customers and employees. Salesforce has long championed pay equity through public wage-gap audits, while Airbnb's leadership has worked directly with local governments to address complex community issues, demonstrating a willingness to engage with challenges rather than avoid them. Each of these companies illustrates a fundamental truth: Leadership is not just about setting direction; it is about ensuring organizations remain open enough to uncover new possibilities and adapt as they move forward.

The same principles apply when working with organizational data. The introduction of generative AI has given teams easier access to information that was previously buried, but that access means little if organizations are unwilling to engage with what they find. Store managers can now use natural language to query data hidden deep in corporate systems, and customer service teams can check local HR and tax regulations across multiple geographies and languages. These are just a few examples of how generative AI has made organizational insights so much more accessible.

However, working with customers during these first infant years of generative AI revealed an interesting pattern: Many organizations deployed models only to become frustrated by the results: "The model is wrong," "This is not correct; why is it saying that?" and so on. But most often, this was not the case. The issue wasn't the model; it was the data. AI was surfacing information that had been hidden deep in the organizational well, often outdated and untouched for years. Forward-looking organizations realized the potential in this and quickly used it as an extra tool to understand what needed to be cleaned up and what should not even be part of the estate anymore. Through this approach and openness to learning with AI, some businesses have not only been able to digitize their operations but also been able to create a sense of contribution and ownership of the new digitized future. This is just uncovering the data.

But if the same principle applies to people, how much knowledge and effort within your teams remains hidden simply because it isn't surfaced? Organizations don't just have data silos—they have human ones, too, and some working actively not to be discovered.

When I worked with Groupe Renault on their transformation, they had a long list of change ideas. Instead of rigidly mapping out every required data point and use case in advance, the team took a learning-based approach. They solved one problem at a time, gradually connecting data like branches growing from a tree. No one could have designed the full system upfront, but over time more and more of the data became interconnected, forming a foundation that could serve a wide range of future use cases. As more data got connected, the ROI increased and the time to delivery often improved. They did not let past organizational hierarchies—whether by brand, function, or process—define the structure. Instead, they shaped their data landscape around the ambition they were driving toward.

At roughly the same time, a competing global company took the opposite approach. They assigned a small group of architects to design their data foundation upfront, carefully mapping out structures before disappearing to build it. Eighteen months later, they unveiled their system—technically correct according to design but disconnected from the realities of the business. By the time it launched, it was already outdated. It had not evolved alongside the organization; nor had it delivered any meaningful value along the way.

The difference between these two approaches underscores a key insight: When organizations build in isolation they risk creating structures that look solid on paper but fail to deliver impact. True progress comes from recognizing that data, like knowledge, isn't static. It has to be uncovered, connected, and continuously shaped to reflect the evolving needs of the business. The same applies to organizational learning—when companies actively invest in openness, challenge assumptions, and use insights to inform action, they don't just digitize operations; they breathe life into ambition, creating a foundation that expands what is possible rather than just keeping pace.

7

ARE YOU CHOOSING TO EXPAND?

I t is said that 90 percent of the thoughts we have in a day are the same as the previous day, which means that change requires an active choice, not just for business but for us as people. Without that choice, it's easy to slip into what some philosophers call "spiritual laziness"—the passive resistance to growth. While opting out of openness and intellectual curiosity might seem harmless, the reality is that complacency has a cost. In business, it leads to stagnation, disengagement, and a failure to recognize emerging opportunities.

The second espresso cup I brought home from Greece had an inscription of a quote by Alexander the Great, "There is nothing impossible to those who will try." I use this cup on days when I need a reminder of the power of persistence and the mindset necessary to drive change. It's a simple but powerful sentiment that speaks to the underlying belief that transformation is possible, even when the odds feel stacked against us. But persistence isn't just about willpower—it's about having the right kind of energy to keep questioning, learning, and adapting.

At a deeper level, the brain is also wired to prioritize avoiding risks over pursuing opportunities. Studies on loss aversion indicate that potential losses feel about twice as impactful as equivalent gains.[1] These instinct shapes what you focus on, how you make decisions, and why you hesitate to challenge what feels certain. Yet research also shows that when you actively engage in learning—when you increase oxygenation and stimulate brain cell growth—you sharpen your ability to problem-solve, reason, and adapt.[2]

Furthermore, we also tend to judge our own actions based on intention, while we judge others based on outcomes. That gap reinforces assumptions, making it even harder to challenge perspectives or fully appreciate alternative viewpoints. Even when the need for change is clear, these natural tendencies—risk aversion, selective judgment, and cognitive shortcuts—can cloud your decisions.

Breaking through this is not about forcing change. Just as with organizations, it is with us. We must create the conditions where new insights actually land, where learning is a constant, where curiosity leads the way, and where better decisions come from seeing the full picture—not just the comfortable one.

It is hard to learn if you already know, so have you actively chosen to change? The openness required for business depends on our courage as leaders and our willingness to face vulnerabilities in order to discover and reveal paths forward. The world will continue to evolve, but your ability to navigate it—and your role within it—comes down to your choice.

RISING TO THE OCCASION

In 2017, when I was at Maersk, the business—like, unfortunately, many others—fell victim to a cyberattack that forced the company to shut down its digital network. For several days, roughly a fifth of global trade was moving without its usual digital backbone. Customers, who normally would delegate their shipping to a junior member of their organization, suddenly had top executives on their toes worrying about ocean shipping at the risk of not receiving their goods. It was akin to the supply chain crunches experienced during the pandemic but on a much bigger scale. All vessels and crews were safe, all cargo was in good care, but we could not provide the answers and updates we normally would.

While crisis management is not foreign in that line of business, this was on a scale no one had planned for. In the midst of system uncertainty and the growing pressure from countless customer production facilities asking questions no one could answer, something happened. Normal structures were disrupted, and decisions started flowing differently. The leaders who were usually expected to have all the answers didn't. Instead, new voices emerged—those closest to the issues were pulled straight into decision-making, not just on the tech side but even more so at the ports, where people accepting trucks and containers had to track goods manually without a system. The leaders with nothing to contribute graciously stepped aside. Ideas surfaced from places they never had before. The openness wasn't just necessary—it was energizing, and solutions were found by the hour. We had nothing, but we found solutions. Every second hour, we managed global phone chains and tight messaging tracks, gathering the relevant information to ensure customers could continue their operations as smoothly as possible. The notes I sent personally twice a day to two million customers with updates on terminal openings weren't perfect, but they were helpful.

Carrying the responsibility of such a large part of the world's global trade without systems to support it could have gone horribly wrong, but the storm was weathered, for the business and for its customers. It showed that true leadership doesn't falter in the face of adversity; it rises to the occasion. The learnings were incredibly valuable. Externally, sharing the challenges increased global awareness of handling of cybersecurity; it tied customer planning closer to business operations. Internally, customer understanding and empathy, as well as the organizational contributions to the solution, became a catalyst for larger change.

In crisis, openness may seem easier. When the data you normally rely on suddenly is not available, being open seems obvious. The curiosity and search alternatives become a driver of sharper, more informed decisions—not indecision. Many leaders had to let go of control, listen, and adapt in real time, watching their organizations step up to the challenge. But what happens when urgency is not forcing change? When there's no immediate pressure to rethink assumptions, do you still challenge the way things are done—or do you default to what is familiar?

I was catching up with a partner at one of the world's largest consulting firms, a firm respected for its talent, expertise, and forward thinking. He shared how the ladder to become partner was so engrained in the business that, despite having access to some of the best global thinking, human behavior was holding back their ability to fully unleash the collective intelligence they had access to. He shared that partners within the firm stored their research on personal laptops, taking it with them when they left, and while collaboration was said to be important, there was no incentive or reward for collaborating. So instead of building one of the world's greatest pools of human strategic thinking, the partners held onto the way it was. The collective value was clear, and while there may have been an impact on the partner rewards, it felt more like asking the fox to guard the henhouse. How many other knowledge firms out there are in the same position? And will they be waiting for disruption or will they step up and lead the change themselves?

A gap like this between a professed desire to invite contribution and the felt reality is not unique. Interestingly, researchers interviewed sixty thousand employees and found that only 14 percent identified leaders with great analytical skills as strong leaders, and 12 percent identified leaders with great social skills (communicative and empathetic) as strong leaders, but 72 percent of teams said great leaders were those who could demonstrate both of these. But of the sample group of leaders, only 1 percent showed this breadth.[3]

Openness is fragile—easily undone by hierarchy, habits, or the instinct to protect what we already know. It is rarely a debate about value or opportunity; more often, it revolves around acceptance of one's own discomforts.

VULNERABILITY OPENS DOORS

Being open means accepting that others' contributions make you stronger. It may seem obvious, yet even the most experienced leaders have moments of thinking, *I can do this best myself.* But how often is that a strategic choice and how often is it a reflex masking something deeper? The need to prove ourselves, a reluctance to rely on others, or a discomfort with letting go—these aren't leadership strengths. They're remnants of past fears dressed as control.

Interestingly, the most common vulnerability among executives is not a skill gap or a blind spot—it is the fear of appearing vulnerable at all. Which is in fact not an actual weakness, but the fear of exposing one. This paradox is what quietly erodes trust, limits collaboration, and narrows decision-making.

The cost, though, is that the tighter the leaders hold on, the more they cut themselves off from the very insights, challenges, and new perspectives that would take them further. Overconfidence creeps in. Risk tolerance drops. But the most dangerous part is that it feels like strength when, in reality, it's a constraint. The best leaders don't remove uncertainty; they create the conditions to navigate it. Vulnerability isn't about *losing* control—it's about having the confidence to open the right doors and let others step in.

> **Vulnerability isn't about *losing* control—it's about having the confidence to open the right doors and let others step in.**

Once a strong leader, since promoted to CEO, stood up in a town hall and said, "I was wrong." It was not a small error but an expensive, thousands-of-manhours, million-dollar learning. The room was silent, waiting for more. But he just repeated himself. He admitted it, and he owned it. He said his decision had been not only wasteful but even occasionally harmful. And he asked for support to change it. Many different looks flew around. But as the whispering quieted down, only a sense of respect and clarity remained. This was a display of leadership that immediately generated followership, and everyone wanted to back him.

The vulnerability of perfectionism is another challenge many leaders face. After all, the quality of their work likely played a role in their rise to the top. But perfectionism—when fueled by fear rather than ambition—can become limiting. In a world with no absolute score for success, clinging to rigid standards can lead to stagnation rather than excellence. The real leadership challenge isn't about stepping away from high standards but rather in shifting from an individual pursuit of perfection to a collective pursuit of excellence. True leadership isn't about proving your own abilities; it's about motivating and unlocking the contributions of others.

I recall an early social gathering just after I had made a career move, where I found myself almost bragging about the talents of my former team—the things they had achieved, the heights they had reached, which far exceeded both their and my own initial expectations. Even though it was true and very impressive, it was not informational—in fact, it was my vulnerabilities talking. This new team and I still had our own mountain to climb, but instead of embracing this, I unconsciously sought to disassociate myself, instead linking myself to the talents and superstars of the past. Years later, I found myself in a similar situation, but this time, my approach had changed. I spoke not about what had been achieved but about what we believed was possible and how we went after it. I focused on the potential of the present team, referencing past experiences only as context, not as a crutch. The situation was nearly identical, but I was not. My vulnerabilities were acknowledged and tempered and no longer disturbed my ability to lead and be inviting to the team.

There are so many business decisions that are influenced by outdated stories in our minds—stories that no longer serve us or have lost their relevance in our current context; experiences, good or bad; and even harmful words that still get carried around and cloud sound business judgment. As leaders, it's essential to examine our vulnerabilities and ask whether they still deserve a voice in our decision-making. Or whether this is, in fact, why we are not reaching higher than we did before.

LEADING WITH EMOTIONAL INTELLIGENCE

The best leaders balance decisiveness with openness, strength with humility, and know and accept their own vulnerabilities. This also means they know that to lead authentically demands both self-regulation and emotional intelligence (EQ). Without EQ, curiosity can turn into a search for validation rather than true exploration.

Emotional intelligence is not just the awareness of your emotions; it is the ability to intelligently use your energy to put things in motion. It encompasses not only emotional awareness but also the ability to leverage emotions effectively in thinking, as well as the ability to regulate and manage these emotions to create energy, cheer, or resilience for yourself and others. Many leaders who neglect the first two elements are not capable of the last and fail to inspire followership.

As with vulnerabilities acknowledging the underlying emotion, its source (versus what society or surroundings may have built it to be) is essential to turn these into strengths. Accepting the emotions and handling and channeling them effectively is not about suppressing emotions but about self-regulating so they don't manage *you*. Spotting a leader with bottled-up emotions is rarely hard to do but can be very hard to bear. Unacknowledged emotions are impossible to use effectively to engage others. Still, some prioritize looking composed over showing what they care about. Perhaps because they have not effectively learned to manage their emotions in a productive way. Leaders who react impulsively, shut down opposing views, or make emotionally driven decisions cut themselves off from benefitting from the collective intelligence and technological advancements of today.

Unlike IQ, EQ is not formally tested in business schools and often not captured within career ladders, despite being a critical leadership differentiator, but it can easily be recognized such as when it comes to those who never admit missteps, dismiss alternative viewpoints, or cannot laugh at themselves. Chances are you have encountered those in leadership with low EQ. They are not only reinforcing their own biases but likely also shutting themselves off from insights that could make them better and their business stronger. Even more so, when you need to win in a platform ecosystem and decompose your product to decide how to deploy and complement it, if emotions cloud your ability to see both your business and the market clearly, the cost can be massive.

In reality, what it would take to change our minds likely lives within our own perceptions and beliefs.

When asked, "What would it take to change your mind?" I have seen leaders jump to search for data points or different contexts. But in reality, what it would take to change our minds likely lives within our own perceptions and beliefs. Expanding is not just about personal openness—it is about embedding that openness in an organization, ensuring that the best ideas are surfaced, tested, and amplified. Believing in collective intelligence—where generative conversations, curiosity, and shared knowledge thrive—is key to unlocking an organization's full potential. This creates value not just within but beyond, as teams no longer wait for leaders to seek external partners. Instead, they actively explore, challenge, and find the strongest contributions to accelerate progress, confidently standing on the shoulders of those already growing and cultivating ecosystems of insight that enable them to reach even further. Choosing to ask ourselves what else could become true is both a personal and a strategic shift. It allows organizations to thrive—not just today but for the long term.

Part II Reflections to Motivate Action: Are You Expanding as You Lead in Motion?

Leadership in motion is meeting change with open eyes, expansive breath, and steady hands—moving with clarity, so others feel ready to step forward with you.

- *Recognized ecosystem value:* What are you doing to ensure the conditions for exponential growth—partnering wisely to grow consciously with others?

- *Expanding with intention and courage:* Which assumptions or routines are narrowing your perspective—and how do you ensure curiosity and openness stay active drivers of better decisions?

- *Rewarding catalytic conversations:* How are you making room for and encouraging conversations in which ideas build on each other—stretching thinking, shaping direction, and moving things forward?

PART III

....

STEERING

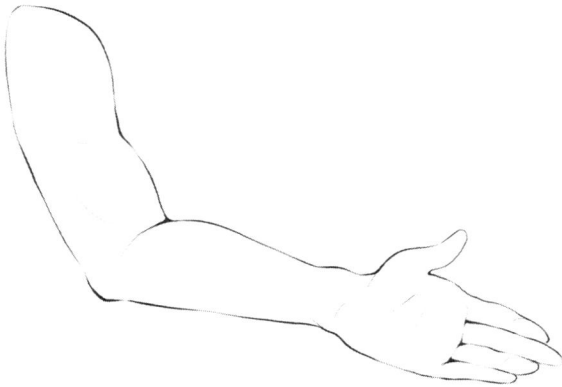

Transformation is about active change. Skilled hands
don't just grasp opportunities—they sculpt direction
by refining rough ideas into deliberate action
and reach out to bring people along.

8

SHAPING MOTION THROUGH
WHAT WE SAY

Visionary ambition and expansive thinking can spark promising ideas, but without efficient steering and making the right adjustments along the way, you risk your organization never becoming a solid, profitable business. Without effective communication, even the most groundbreaking strategies struggle to take root, let alone thrive.

In fact, communication inconsistency can slash business performance by more than 30 percent, according to Dorian Stone, cofounder of McKinsey's Global Customer Experience practice.[1] This is not just about the risk of miscommunication; it is about the very essence of your ambition, strategy, and leadership becoming diluted, distorted, or even completely lost.

Take, for instance, WeWork—where a compelling and grand ambition was not matched by the operational discipline, governance, and clarity needed to build a resilient business. The CEOs vision-driven rhetoric rang hollow and sent contradicting signals to employees and investors. When questioned, he was not able to listen and take challenge as inspiration to improve. He eventually left, and the business later had to file for bankruptcy. On another scale, but probably even more in the public eye, Boeing's initial slow and defensive handling of their safety challenges in 2018 and 2019 with one aircraft was followed by operational challenges and labor strikes in 2024. Their communication was in large part reactive and vague, and as a result, significant revenue-share price and reputational decline followed. This also led to a change in CEO.

It is therefore not surprising to see that the skill in highest demand today, based on all positions posted on LinkedIn in the past year, is communication.[2] The largest growth in roles are those in AI and tech, but the most sought-after competencies are communication, emotional intelligence, creativity and innovation, decision-making, adaptability, and critical thinking. It is powerful to see the recognition of these skills, especially when acknowledging that communication, emotional intelligence, and adaptability are key drivers of critical thinking and decision-making.

COMMUNICATION AS AN ANCHOR

Navigating change and ensuring that every message and every interaction reinforces a consistent forward momentum is key. But how can you still represent a clear and compelling voice to follow in a world of venturing, empowerment, and ecosystems—where all the clear steps ahead are therefore not yet defined?

It involves consistently reinforcing and inspiring confidence in the ambition, creating space for teams to contribute and see themselves within it. It requires demonstrating accountability by leading decisively, respectfully, and responsibly toward outcomes.

Apple's Think Different campaign was a masterclass in communication—simple, powerful, and deeply resonant. It didn't just promote a product; it invited people into a mindset, challenging them to break from the status quo and embrace creativity. More than marketing, it was a call to action that built loyalty and shaped how people viewed technology.

Crucially, Apple's leaders ensured the message was not just words—their products embodied the same boldness. Every innovation, from design to functionality, reinforced the ambition in a way that felt real and actionable. This is our role as leaders: not just to articulate a vision but to set the tone, create alignment, ensure that actions reflect the message, and make it real for those we seek to inspire.

Striking the right balance between conviction and openness does more than set a direction, it invites teams to co-own the journey. While clarity and confidence are essential leadership qualities, they can also create unintended barriers. When communication feels too authoritative, it may signal certainty rather than openness, making it harder for others to challenge ideas or offer alternative perspectives. If people feel alienated—whether by rigid decision-making, dismissive communication, or a lack of receptiveness—they are less likely to contribute, weakening the collective intelligence of the team.

I was making a major move, leaving a successful career chapter in one industry behind to step into another. As I left, a talented employee of mine gave me a piece of advice: "Wear your hair down on the first day." I smiled and thanked her but didn't follow it. I was, after all, joining a very operational, male-dominated environment. In hindsight, it was the perfect advice. She knew I would be sharp, direct, and determined to deliver, but she also knew that these traits alone would not immediately show my warmth, my openness to partnership, or my willingness to learn. By not following her advice, I may have appeared competitive rather than complementary, potentially missing out on valuable collaborative opportunities. I had neglected the power of that advice and insight about how my leadership presence sometimes makes teams feel they aren't invited to truly contribute. True leadership is about cultivating an environment where contributions are welcomed and valued.

Accountability in transformation is not about having all the answers from the start—it is about making decisions that create clarity, even in uncertainty. By design, transformation means moving forward without a full blueprint of the complete future market, and as leaders, we must make calls based on incomplete information, remove distractions to reveal what truly drives impact, and adjust as needed. Deferring tough decisions doesn't maintain stability—it deepens ambiguity and shifts the burden onto those already stretched, forcing them to navigate uncertainty without direction. Too often teams have read the patterns of change long before any company-wide message comes out, and the vacuum this creates just lowers engagement, demotivates, and slows down change. It is your responsibility to constantly shape the trajectory of change through communication. Owning both the planned and the unexpected is not about controlling every outcome—it's about recognizing when to provide clarity, when to recalibrate, and when to let the organization process and adapt. In transformation, communication is not just about delivering a message—it is about ensuring that message is absorbed, understood, and acted on.

As with all communication, when driving change, the starting point must always be to meet people where they are. Within businesses, I have seen investments in training to build common vocabulary to foster increased respect and understanding for different functions and domains. While this strengthens complementary thinking and shared value articulation, it is important to remember that the goal is not to become someone else but to meet them where they are and invite them to the shared future you seek.

This reminds me of a story that may not fully match here but clearly underscores the power of change by meeting people where they are. When the gin Bombay Sapphire was launched by Diageo, it was created with a very special objective: It was specifically designed to appeal to vodka drinkers seeking something new yet familiar. Many had a desire to shift to gins that had a more sophisticated perception, but they did not feel comfortable. By using visual cues such as a color that reminded them of vodka packaging, while highlighting gin's botanical sophistication in the Bombay Sapphire packaging, the brand gradually led vodka consumers into a new experience without overwhelming them. The taste was equally subdued, yet it carried nuances of spice. Consumers loved it. They felt safe yet excited to take a bold move forward. And we managed to move them subtly.

Effective change communication builds a bridge between the known and the new. Even when a clear strategic vision is set and signposted, the subsequent communication can, with benefit, highlight the step-by-step contributions included in the journey toward the ambition. Focusing on these smaller, tangible wins serves as proof points of progress, reinforcing confidence and motivation to keep moving forward. While strategy benefits from being crafted with a future-back approach, communication must also be anchored in a present-forward perspective.

ASYNCHRONOUS STAKEHOLDER MANAGEMENT

Equal to communication as an anchor, I would never underestimate the value of progress over perfection. As the organization is moving as an organism, it is clear that the flow and pace are really what matters. I have also experienced firsthand how this can sometimes be hard to swallow, but in the grand journey of change, it is easily forgotten once momentum accelerates.

In pursuit of greater customer understanding in a large operational business, the team and I were launching a company-wide aligned customer segmentation. It was a classic situation where sales teams had their priorities, marketing had another, and operations had yet a different lens to decide who to prioritize and not. Going into this everyone was happy with their own lens on things, until we started exposing the inconsistencies and costs that teams were inadvertently creating for each other and the wasted efforts taken to mitigate this lack of alignment. People started to at least be willing to entertain the conversation.

We mapped the market, not our market, but the total market. We brought in data, quantitative and qualitative, and investigated needs and behaviors. We held several workshops to identify patterns and involve teams in the creation and from this develop a framework, which helped us all understand and serve customers more effectively. Importantly, it created a common frame of reference and enabled us to establish a governance that ensured that customers within a certain segment were treated equally by all departments in the company.

At one point in the process, a senior executive walked into one of the workshops and looked at the large whiteboard on the wall, where we had diligently captured the framework with the various customer needs and behaviors and clusters forming. He grabbed a pen and drew a triangle on top of it. The truth was our data did not align with a triangle—the clusters were spread widely across a grid. However, the simplicity and conviction of his message won followership. The risk of not gaining buy-in outweighed the technical precision of the visual.

It was as if the penny had dropped for many, and suddenly this became the new way forward. Debates shifted to underlying layers, such as the number of segments—some argued for fewer, some for more to capture nuances, and others advocated for micro-segmentation. But the goal was not precision—it was forward movement. This helped people grasp the concept, and shifting from no aligned customer understanding to a shape that people could remember brought the organization to a shared trajectory. It meant that unaligned efforts could be saved and that the most profitable business could be served better in an aligned approach across the business. As a result, the company invested time in bringing these segments to life through names, personifications, and storytelling, ensuring they were memorable and relatable even in operational settings. It created a common language and identity, alignment, and momentum.

Over time, more and more people naturally saw that the triangle was not representative, but at this stage, the business had moved on, and the vocabulary of the underlying segments and behaviors was engrained, and the triangle could disappear from all material.

This process wasn't just about analysis and alignment—it was a form of organizational dialogue. The way ideas were introduced, sequenced, and absorbed mattered as much as their accuracy. Pacing shaped engagement; had we insisted on full precision too early, the effort might have collapsed under its own weight. Instead, providing a structure people could grasp allowed them to process complexity in stages. The triangle, though flawed, acted as a bridge—a shared reference that moved the conversation forward until the real substance took root. Change does not happen in a single moment of clarity; it gains traction when people have the space to engage with it, internalize it, and make it their own.

Another recurring challenge with transformations is the gap between the board narrative and reality. The glossy story crafted to gain support and backing for investments versus the felt change for teams and customers. I have always encouraged my teams to read the public announcements and, if possible, board minutes to learn to decode the pressures leaders face. This not only helps them align their contributions but also creates opportunities to surface their progress toward the ambition. It is also a simple way to invite contributions from below the surface.

> Change does not happen in a single moment of clarity; it gains traction when people have the space to engage with it, internalize it, and make it their own.

At the same time, leaders must own that clarity and consistency. An executive recently shared a conversation with his majority shareholder, who expected immediate organic growth without investment, while he was on the path to a much more valuable and larger-scale transformation. He felt the pressure, and inevitably, his team did, too. Too often, I encounter situations where, in an attempt to shield teams, leaders unknowingly create gaps in communication, causing pressure to be felt downward without the full context being shared. When communication becomes asynchronous at different levels of the organization, the energy that should fuel progress instead turns into unnecessary speculation and, at worst, friction.

Clear and consistent communication turns leadership pressure into momentum rather than confusion. While teams can seek to understand strategic intent, as leaders we must create transparency to ensure alignment, not ambiguity.

Similarly, I have experienced external communication take a huge toll on the value of a transformation. Typically, in more transformative change, the investors lose their reference peer group and even the most powerful transformation can be underestimated, leading to unnecessary scrutiny and pressure on the leaders. I have seen bold moves where companies suddenly declare themselves tech companies, which may indeed represent the vision, spark good debate, and attract talent, but also creates expectations for the ability to show margins that resemble a tech company. Or lately, the amount of companies that handle data and now claim to be AI companies is astonishing, and where indeed there may be a small element of truth to their claims, I expect the next few years will expose those who have merely adopted the label without the underlying capability, leading to tough recalibration when results fail to align with the narrative. Just as owning a pair of sneakers does not make you a professional athlete, using AI to support your business does not make you an AI company. Companies who, on the other hand, succeed in managing this well are the ones who take responsibility and understand that it is their job to create excitement with the progress and comfort with the journey taken, also for the external audience.

An example of managing investor relations well was when Microsoft made the strategic shift toward cloud computing. CEO Satya Nadella early on communicated a vision, both in the form of products and in terms of culture, and managed to consistently demonstrate progress toward it. This supported Microsoft in the following years in significantly exceeding the share price growth of the S&P500 and Nasdaq, as well as that of the then-incumbent cloud player AWS. They were able to transcend both their old and new peer groups.

So just like managing growth in venturing is a constant balance between inspiring with the ambition and recognizing the immediate steps taken, so is the rhythm with communication. It is about staying one step ahead but never so far that you lose the audience—stretching the horizon without breaking the link.

SOMATIC MARKERS OF CHANGE

While strategy sets the direction, communication builds the path for people to follow.

Sometimes, people need to see change, not just hear about it. Small, often-overlooked cues—what we might call "somatic markers"—signal transformation in ways words cannot. Businesses have long understood this, using everything from office layouts to dress codes and partnerships to reinforce cultural shifts. These signals don't just shape perception; they shape behavior, influencing how people engage with change.

The smallest shifts can carry unexpected weight. I've seen leadership teams' debate over the removal of neckties last longer than those over an investment, and rightly so—not because of the fabric but because unwritten rules provide comfort. Change, even when welcome, can feel disorienting if people are not sure what will replace the old norms. A company shifting from a rigid hierarchy to a more agile structure might remove formal titles, but without clear alternatives, people struggle to navigate influence and decision-making.

This is because change that evokes emotion leaves a stronger imprint. Research shows that intense emotional experiences stimulate neuron growth and strengthen connections in the brain.[3] The more vivid and emotionally charged an event, the more likely it is to be remembered.[4] This is why shared experiences—positive or negative—can bond teams together and make transformations feel real rather than theoretical. When organizations fail to create tangible, emotional markers of change, people struggle to internalize it.

Consider Natura & Co, the Latin American beauty giant that transformed itself into a global sustainability leader. Its acquisition of the Body Shop and Avon was not just about business expansion—it reinforced its environmental and ethical positioning. This shift was made tangible—packaging changed to emphasize sustainability, store experiences highlighted eco-friendly commitments, and internal culture was reshaped to align with purpose-driven leadership. Employees and customers did not just hear about the transformation—they experienced it in every interaction.

Similarly, when Huawei wanted to move beyond its lower-cost alternative, it didn't just improve its products; it signaled a shift in ambition by partnering with Porsche—not just for brand association but to anchor a new premium identity in the market.

Transformation is not just about strategy—it is about embodiment. Leaders must show, not tell, what change looks like—because if people don't see it, feel it, and experience it, they likely will not believe it.

STEERING AHEAD WITH CLEAR COMMUNICATION

Transformation is not just about intellectual shifts—it is deeply rooted in the emotional and cultural contexts that shape how we experience change. Success depends not only on what is said but on how and when it is communicated.

Finding common ground in global business goes far beyond data and strategy; it requires an understanding of the cultural nuances that influence decision-making, trust, and engagement. The most effective strategies bridge business objectives with what genuinely matters to the people they aim to serve and those who are responsible for delivering it.

Too often, communication gets lost in translation, not because the message itself is wrong, but because it fails to consider the emotional and cultural context in which it is received. Imagine a worker in a warehouse: He knows where the safety lines are, he has access to the right tools, and he understands the procedures. But he is also aware that the business is behind schedule. He knows that if he runs just a little faster, his boss will be less grumpy. If he steps out for a quick cigarette behind the entrance door instead of the designated area, he will get back faster. He may even skip a step to get through the tasks faster and finish early to spend just a few more minutes with his child. None of these decisions are made out of negligence—they are human choices balancing efficiency pressure and personal priorities.

This is where accidents happen, not because procedures are not in place, but because human nature fills in the gaps between rules and reality. When left unnoticed, small deviations accumulate to systematic risks. It is not just physical accidents that result from cutting corners; it is the emotional toll that builds when things do not go as planned or when people feel overwhelmed.

I once experienced this firsthand when a colleague—a leader I deeply respected—pulled me aside and said, "You know, you don't smile anymore." For me, this was very off-character. It was not criticism; it was an observation. But at that moment, I realized how much my own stress had become a silent signal to my team. My focus had been on managing change, but I had failed to recognize how my own demeanor shaped the energy of those around me. It is easy sometimes to lose sight of your emotional balance, but in doing so, you risk losing connection with those you lead because leadership is as much about the emotions you project as the strategies you drive.

As leaders, we must continuously tune into both the intellectual and the emotional readiness of our teams, ensuring they meet each other where they are, bridging gaps, relieving concerns, reminding them of the ambition, and reinforcing direction—because in communication, just as in venturing, when contributions come from all directions, the narrative can easily drift too far from reality. Small deviations will inevitably emerge, and leaders must be acutely aware of them—assessing whether they are surprising and valuable accelerators to be amplified, misunderstood shortcuts that need guidance, or distractions that should be shut down. If left unaddressed, these shifts can gradually lead teams further from the intended path—and, perhaps more critically, further from the leader. On the other hand, when transformation communication is stewarded with intent, teams internally and externally navigate change with confidence. Change becomes not just

> **When transformation communication is stewarded with intent, teams internally and externally navigate change with confidence.**

accepted but embraced, and transformation becomes a shared journey in which everyone can contribute and thrive.

A leader who leads decisively, respectfully, and responsibly doesn't just manage change; they shape its trajectory, clear the path for those delivering it, and take ownership of the outcomes—both planned and unexpected. Great leaders don't just navigate transformation; they make it possible for others to engage in. They understand that change doesn't happen in a vacuum; it requires an emotional and cultural foundation that allows people to process, participate, and ultimately believe in the transformation. The best leaders increase their teams' capacity for change by ensuring they don't just survive it but thrive within it. It is your responsibility to ensure that journey is one people are invited to join—not just to follow.

9

THE PULSE OF CHANGE

I magine a group of people on a hill. Music is playing. One man is dancing. He is happy but to others probably looks a bit crazy. He's a bit of a loner but not bothered by that fact. People notice him. Some laugh and some shake their heads—much as in a corporate setting with the challengers. This is shown in a YouTube viral video captured in 2009.[1] It is a good and much-seen video. It speaks to the important concept of followership. It also reminds us that leadership is not about titles or tenure—it's about how you show up and the impact you generate.

What the video brilliantly depicts is a first mover demonstrating something new, and then a crucial and brave person joining him, emulating the first person's moves. Consequently, the first person instantly becomes more respected, and they together start showing a way for others to consider. The person who joined the first mover has shown that this is okay to take part, and soon more join to form a crowd and soon enough a movement has started. This is no longer about the first mover, as they all now co-own the movement, and bystanders can see the value of inclusion, which can quickly be gained. This great illustration shows that driving change is all about derisking change and creating stages for all to join in at the level where they feel comfortable. Some will be first movers, some will be fast followers, and some will only come when the masses do. Value them all, but know who is who so you don't waste your efforts.

Just like the lone dancer who sparked a movement, driving change in an organization requires understanding the dynamics of followership and creating an environment where people feel safe to join in. In fact, driving change is truly about reading and working with the organization's nervous system. Change will be inflicted at the macro, meso, or micro levels. While some people read businesses based on their numbers, structures, and processes, to manage meaningful change, I find it most important to understand and predict human motivations and interactions. Fortunately, good employees inherently want to contribute to their leaders' success, so ensuring a strong two-way understanding of expectations and motivations creates alignment without the need for control.

The easy starting point is to look at the unwritten dynamics of leadership—the rhythm of decision-making, the formats in which executives best receive input, and their personal styles. Does the CEO prefer to reflect in solitude over the weekend, expecting the team to catch the key decisions on Monday? Are decisions made collaboratively, or do multiple stakeholders compete to influence the outcome? Understanding these nuances can make all the difference, and if your teams have not caught onto decoding this, tell them! No need to waste energy on not being aligned here. And as always, be open to alternative suggestions.

PERSONAL DRIVERS OF CHANGE

One of the most valuable strategies for managing transformation is understanding what personally drives key stakeholders. This goes beyond tracking tasks or schedules—it is about recognizing the different levels of motivation that shape how people engage with change. While some are eager to move forward, others may be assessing what the shift means for their security, role, or sense of belonging. Respecting these differences is key to building momentum.

Not all motivations are equal. Extrinsic rewards—such as salary increases, bonuses, or promotions—can provide short-term incentives, but they rarely create lasting commitment. Studies on self-determination theory have shown that while financial incentives can enhance performance in structured, repetitive tasks, they often diminish creativity, adaptability, and problem-solving—the very qualities needed in transformation.[2] When change demands new thinking and initiative, extrinsic rewards alone can lead to short-term compliance rather than genuine engagement. Long-term commitment comes from deeper drivers—personal growth, fulfillment, and a sense of contribution—reinforcing the value of a strongly lead venturing model. Some individuals seek clarity on how they can navigate an evolving landscape without losing their sense of identity, while others look for opportunities to expand their influence and impact.

In times of uncertainty, not all foundational needs—such as security, belonging, and esteem—can be fully met. Yet you can still foster a sense of agency and inclusion through communication, ownership, and ambition. When people are informed, have a stake in decisions, and can see how their role contributes to a larger ambition, they are less likely to experience change as a personal risk. Instead, they find their place within it, strengthening both their confidence and their ability to contribute.

Change moves at different speeds for different people. The pulse of change is about not just setting a vision but tuning it in to the motivations that determine whether people engage, resist, or lead the way forward. As leaders, we can make these assessments in the moment, but a more strategic approach—often in collaboration with trusted partners—yields deeper insights and more effective outcomes. Drawing from my experience, I have always made this one of the most important responsibilities of my executive assistants, working together on powerful analysis of stakeholders' willingness to change, leveraging hard data—such as board schedules, financial results, and organizational shifts—and softer insights. This has made managing change much more effective, when I was extra conscious of, for example, whether the person I was going to meet next was likely to be energized or drained from their prior engagements. Or were they an introvert who had just given a public speech and might need a mental break? Understanding these nuances allowed me to tailor my approach more effectively, improving our chances of generative conversations and accelerating change.

The pulse of change is about not just setting a vision but tuning it in to the motivations that determine whether people engage, resist, or lead the way forward.

Like most learnings, this starts with listening and clever observation, not just to words but more so to the underlying context and emotions. Earlier in my career, I used to continuously invite myself to meetings—something I am sure many emerging talents can relate to. My boss at the time would kindly laugh about my habit, and while I am sure I was a bit annoying, it was not only about gathering business information. That part could be read in the minutes, but it was much more about observing how people operated and reacted to messages. Who sought validation through shared laughter? Who only spoke when prompted? Who monopolized time? Who commented on other teams' work? It was about reading the people, the unspoken dynamics, and understanding their desires, fears, and motivations. These subtle cues helped me better understand what made them tick and, ultimately, how to align with their motivations to drive change. Some might call this a frivolous use of time, but experience has proven otherwise. My ability to decode a room quickly now—sometimes in seconds—is an invaluable skill in driving change. And even more importantly, when we as leaders train our ability to decode and understand the deeper motivations behind what people say and do, we become more effective at fueling our team's motivations.

At an organizational level, this extends beyond individual leaders. Managing motivation across teams is just as critical as managing strategy. Knowing when to push forward and when to create space for reflection ensures that momentum is sustained rather than forced. Just as individuals need time to process and adapt in their own ways, not all resistance is loud; in fact, most is not. But seeing teams disengage quietly, doing what is asked without investing in the outcome or waiting for certainty before moving forward, is a huge cost. I am sure you know who these people are around you. The cost is not only to the business but also to the individuals, who dwindle over time through a loss of sense of purpose and impact. When motivation is lacking, busyness will likely show, but even the best strategy won't translate into action.

YOU CAN'T PLANT SEEDS IN FROSTY GROUND

Change only takes hold when people are ready, and forcing it rarely leads to anything but resistance. One of the most important lessons I am reminded of time and time again is that you can't plant seeds in frosty ground. But when the ground is frozen, no amount of watering will make the seeds grow; it will only make the ground harder. Pushing against resistance doesn't break down barriers; it only hardens them.

In my early career, I believed that with enough effort, everyone could be motivated to change. But if you believe this, there is a risk that the price will be highest on yourself. Just like the story about the group of executives assessing the value of cloud technology, where the brave leader quietly shared that it was their own remaining tenure and risk of not being personally successful that held them back. They were not resisting out of stubbornness—they had made a deliberate calculation to stay frozen for a few more years. No amount of pressure that day would have changed their stance, but it was still a valuable data point on their journey. And one that hopefully contributed to the fact that a few of them are now finding other paths to ensure their own strong legacy. This was about tapping into their process, not mine, so maybe that meeting was just one small step on their defrosting journey after all.

One must be ready to catch people when there are small signs of defrosting. These, in my experience, are best found in the softer signals— the passing comments, the subtle shift in body language, the quiet curiosity that was not there before. They are always tied to something personal: a moment of realization, a shift in priorities, or an internal question that was not present before. Sometimes, it is not about embracing change fully but about finding a part of it that resonates—an angle that feels relevant to them. Recognizing these moments requires patience, but it does not have to take time. It is about attentiveness, the ability to sense when the ice is beginning to crack and knowing how to extend a soft nonjudgmental hand before it freezes over again.

Redirecting energy to more fertile ground while people defrost is not a failure; it is a strategic move. It is essential to identify who is ready for change and who is not and rather than exhausting energy on the most resistant, start with those who are showing signs of openness. Investing effort in those who are unwilling to engage too soon can drain momentum and create unnecessary strain. Manage around them; get others to defrost, to move, and to experience how change becomes contagious. Once a few start moving, it becomes easier for those who need to see the crowd move before they follow.

Certainly, owners can force change or bosses can push change, but this is not defrosting; it is just compliance. Before I learned this, many years ago, I was trying to push change too intensely. The ambition was right, but my pace was wrong. And when others slowed down from disengagement, I just increased my acceleration to compensate. I was doing something *to* them, instead of with them and for them. Instead of creating momentum, I just widened the gap. My completely new boss at the time was trying to help me see this and suggested that I take a yoga class. While the advice probably came from a well-intended place, my ground was frosty, and instead it landed with me as sexist and strange. Why would I slow down when I was only trying to deliver exactly what the business needed?

Still, determined to do whatever it took, I booked a yoga class. And I completely missed the point. Every time the instructor said *breathe*, my mind rushed to: *Is the instructor crazy? If I was not breathing, I would be dead by now.* I treated it like a competition—stretching as far as possible, executing every move technically right—but without embodying it. I was there, but not present. I went through the motions, wasted the hour, and gained nothing from it.

It is the same with any transformation effort. A well-intended leader can send their teams on the best training courses, introduce new tools, or implement change initiatives, but if the individuals involved are not open to engaging, the effort is lost. At best, it is forgotten. At worst, it builds frustration. This is because change is not just about exposure—it is about receptivity, and receptivity does not happen because someone tells us to engage. It happens when we see others moving with us, making space for us to step into change rather than pushing us toward it. Especially as leaders, we must show, not tell.

At that point in my career, I had not yet grasped how to manage the pulse of change. I was too focused on the ones standing still rather than the ones who were already starting to shift. But once I understood, everything changed. When the right people start moving together, change stops being something to push and starts being something that pulls others along. And the numbers support this. Companies with highly engaged teams see a 20 percent increase in productivity and a 21 percent boost in profitability.[3]

This isn't just about motivation—it's about how brains respond to change. Research has shown that exposure alone does not drive adaptation; engagement does, but engagement is social. Pioneering studies on neuroplasticity found that when environments introduce new stimuli, cognitive capacity expands, but when individuals are surrounded by novelty yet remain disengaged, growth stalls.[4] Change is not just about introducing something new; it is about making change feel like a shared movement. The same applies to organizations. You can introduce change, but if your teams do not see it as something others are already leaning into, resistance builds, structures stay rigid, and momentum is lost.

By understanding the human side of change, you can unlock a wellspring of motivation and create a more sustainable and fulfilling path forward—one that is not only effective but also a rewarding journey of discovery, for both the organization and the individuals within it.

MOBILIZING WITH EXTERNAL WAKES

A former colleague of mine came from an earlier job in the BBC newsroom, and he taught me a valuable lesson—one that is critical when steering change: the great value of an editorial mindset. Newsrooms thrive on anticipation. By analyzing data signals, they predict upcoming events and align their content accordingly. This proactive approach ensures they remain relevant and engaging to their audience. They don't just react to events; they anticipate, shape, and position themselves ahead of the story.

With the sheer volume of data available today, this mindset should no longer be exclusive to newsrooms—it should be a fundamental part of how leaders navigate change. The ability to track patterns, read signals, and anticipate what will matter next is just as critical in business as it is in journalism. It enables businesses to reap benefits and shape their trajectory.

But navigating change is not just about looking outward—it is also about understanding how an organization structures itself to act on what it sees. The most effective transformations operate at three levels: macro, meso, and micro.

- The macro level is where leaders engage with big-picture shifts: What tectonic changes are occurring in the industry, and how does the organization want to position itself?

- The micro level is the granular, day-to-day execution: What decisions, initiatives, and actions move the organization forward?

- The meso level in between—arguably the most crucial—is where the complexity of transformation plays out. This is where an organization's structures, teams, and systems interconnect to interpret macro shifts and guide micro-level action.

  The meso level is what allows an organization to move from recognizing external wakes to actually mobilizing in response. It ensures that a company does not just react sporadically but instead builds internal alignment that enables real impact. A newsroom doesn't just chase breaking stories (micro) or set broad editorial priorities (macro)—it also orchestrates workflows, beats, and resource allocation (meso) to ensure it captures and contextualizes events effectively. Similarly, businesses must balance strategic foresight with structured execution, and that happens at the meso level.

Large-scale change often comes from a dynamic interplay of three pivotal external forces: people, money, and legislation. These forces, while distinct, are deeply interconnected, creating the external conditions that define whether change gains momentum or stalls—and the best change leaders know how to read them, catch them, and mobilize them for their own transformation.

They can reshape markets by introducing disruptive innovations (such as the rise of smartphones, fueled by consumer demand and venture capital) or shifting consumer behaviors (e.g., the growing interest in sustainable products). They redefine norms by challenging established practices (such as the shift toward hybrid work) and force leaders to take a stance on critical matters (such as dialogues about diversity, equity, and inclusion). They can present openings for organizations to align their transformation with the waves that markets create.

However, these forces can also present unexpected challenges, forcing organizations to confront unforeseen obstacles. The broadest-reaching in recent memory was the COVID-19 pandemic, but trade tariffs and regulatory shifts are equally changing the game for many as of the time of this writing. And yet most of the change we are experiencing today was proclaimed earlier—we simply chose not to build hypotheses around it. Mastering reading the interplay of people, money, and legislation is essential but not simple. It requires recognizing their synergistic potential while also anticipating points of friction. For instance, tapping into evolving consumer desires (people) can unlock opportunities for strategic investment (money) and even pave the way for favorable regulations (legislation). That is a powerful way for leaders to manage the pulse of change and steer transformations to success.

Consider the semiconductor and chip market: The rising user interest in AI, automation, and computing power (people) has fueled massive investment in chip manufacturing and innovation (money). Now, legislation is actively shaping the landscape, with the US CHIPS Act and Europe's semiconductor strategy injecting billions (money) into domestic production to reduce reliance on Asia (legislation). At the same time, dependencies on raw materials, geopolitical tensions, and export controls (legislation) are disrupting supply chains, forcing companies to rethink strategies overnight. The scarcity and uneven distribution of raw materials, coupled with rising demand, have driven up prices, spurred intense competition, and reallocated investments (money). This has led to new legislative initiatives (legislation) promoting sustainable mining practices and establishing strategic reserves, driven by concerns from businesses and consumers (people).

Companies with a strong meso-level structure are able to position themselves at the center of these industry realignments. TSMC and Nvidia secured key roles in global supply chains and captured investment ahead of policy-driven constraints. Google recognized the risk of dependence and was fast at developing its own chips to support AI platforms and gain control over supply. Meanwhile, Tata Electronics, part of the Indian conglomerate, quickly moved into this space, establishing India's first indigenous semiconductor assembly and test facility in Assam. This aligned with India's semiconductor policy (legislation) and aimed to reduce dependence on foreign chip supplies.

Without a cohesive meso-level response, even companies aware of macro trends can struggle with micro-level execution. A market opportunity alone does not translate into success—organizational alignment and the ability to execute across interconnected teams determine whether an opportunity turns into a competitive advantage.

People at scale are a force that is difficult to overturn—one that the tech industry, in particular, has been very good at mobilizing. Consider TikTok, which rapidly reshaped social media consumption patterns by capturing a generation's attention and redefining engagement—forcing incumbents such as Meta and YouTube to adapt their platforms in response. Or Stripe, which did not just offer a payment solution but fundamentally changed how digital transactions were processed, pushing traditional banks to rethink their infrastructure. Similarly, Airbnb and Uber gained mass consumer support by turning underutilized assets—homes and cars—into competitive alternatives to established industries, disrupting hotels and taxi services beyond what regulators and industry leaders had anticipated. Once people mobilize, change happens.

Markets that over-rely on legislation stifle innovation, leaving leaders stunned when disruption hits. Conversely, proactive legislation can create entirely new industries. The emergence of the internet and e-commerce, for example, was significantly influenced by legislation like the US Telecommunications Act of 1996, which deregulated the industry and fostered competition. This led to massive investment in online businesses and a fundamental shift in consumer behavior.

To read investment patterns effectively, curious leaders look beyond where capital is flowing—they analyze the pace, source, and underlying strategic intent. Capital inflows signal industry momentum, but sustained growth depends on whether funding is speculative or tied to structural shifts. Sectors flooded with venture capital not only experience rapid expansion but also face volatility when funding dries up. And if one has not managed to mobilize, for instance, people, success rarely lasts. Established institutional investments, on the other hand, support long-term confidence.

Some say that sudden surges in funding often precede industry restructuring, while capital slowdowns can expose fragile business models—a good time not to be slow on your transformation. Executives who track these movements and curiously listen to economists—not just the headlines—gain an edge in anticipating shifts before they fully unfold.

Individually, each of these forces—people, money, and legislation—shapes industries. But their real power lies in how they interact. Markets move fastest when all three forces align, when consumer demand is met with investment and reinforced by regulation. On the other hand, misalignment between these forces can create market failures. If investment outpaces demand, bubbles form and collapse. If regulation resists change, industries stagnate while innovation moves elsewhere. All these levers of change—product evolution, market dynamics, regulatory shifts—show up in data. To effectively mobilize external wakes and manage the pulse of transformation, you must keep your lens on the patterns of people, money, and legislation—and ensure that your macro, meso, and micro responses remain in sync. Markets don't wait for companies to be ready. The forces shaping industries are in motion—whether businesses act on them or not.

> **As emotionally in tune as leaders must be about driving human and organizational change, they must be equally unemotional in reading the forces shaping markets.**

The question is: Are you steering these forces to your advantage, or are you being pulled along by them? A strong ability to drive change at the meso level is often what allows organizations to pace their response and turn external forces into opportunities. I have seen this done well when businesses have a deep understanding of their products' potential, their configurability, and their broader relevance—without being locked into current value streams. When organizations approach change with this level of adaptability, they don't just react to shifts—they position themselves ahead of them.

As emotionally in tune as leaders must be about driving human and organizational change, they must be equally unemotional in reading the forces shaping markets. And the exciting thing about the man dancing on the hill was not him, or the crowd that formed later, but the transitions—the moments where the context shifts and we have an opportunity to lean in, redefine, and decide our roles. If you lose yourself in transitions, you will lose yourself in transformations.

10

STAFFING FOR WHAT
YOU WISH TO ACHIEVE

We know that leaders play a crucial role in ensuring the right environment, resources, and mindset for change to succeed. But are you surrounded by the right people to succeed? There is a story I heard about a group of apes in a zoo who got sprayed with uncomfortably cold water any time one of them took a banana from the corner of their enclosure. The troop quickly learned the pattern and reprimanded any ape who tried to take a banana, because none of them wanted the uncomfortable punishment. One by one, the apes were changed to the point where none of the apes in the zoo had ever even experienced the cold water, but they had seen the apes before them punish anyone who went for the banana. So the behavior continued. This is an anecdote often linked back to G. R. Stephenson's research from 1967[1] and is often used as an analogy for humans and social conditioning. Not only is personal change difficult; mobilizing groups to move requires active orchestration.

Then there's the famous quote that speaks to the sentiment of insanity being defined as doing the same thing repeatedly and expecting different results. Yet too often, organizations fall into this trap. A well-intentioned initiative, perhaps launched with enthusiasm and a detailed kickoff, falls short of its desired outcomes because the organizational structures and mindsets remain unchanged. Just as we tend to overestimate our own skills, the same can be the case when looking at the organizations we are responsible for. This is great when building conviction in venturing but can create a serious misunderstanding of capacities. In fact, data from Korn Ferry says that 94 percent of leaders expect to pick up a new skill on the job.[2] Imagine you have identified a great ambition, you have enabled contributions from within and across the ecosystem, and more than nine out of ten of your own teams acknowledge they need to learn new skills. How fast do you think change will happen?

"Act as you wish to be perceived" has long been a piece of advice given to upcoming talent, but why do so many businesses still then staff for the past? It is leadership's responsibility to manage this to profitable success, so are the necessary moves being made?

One of the biggest barriers to staffing for transformation is reluctance—not just at the leadership level but across the organization. Considering the time and effort to bring new talent well into an organization and the cost of cultural assimilation—not to mention the rational argument of short-term staff change costs, potential union considerations, and the investment and challenges of upskilling employees who have the drive but lack the necessary skills—the hesitation is understandable. Furthermore, these costs are often more tangible and visible than the opportunity cost of change. Yet it is still striking how many businesses invest heavily in transformation costs elsewhere while neglecting one of the most fundamental levers of change: people.

This was the center of a conversation I had with a chairman of the board of a Fortune 500 company. We were completely aligned on what role strategically placed individuals would signal in the right change. We could clearly see how a specific, well-respected individual with strong clout, strategic acumen, and followership would not only move the business multiple steps forward but also propel him forward as a leader of change. However, the chairman declined to encourage his executive management team to do it. He said, "They are still evaluating promotions through traditional levers, and we would be doing this talent a disservice." Sad but true. This example illustrates a common pitfall: Even when a company intellectually recognizes the need for change, deeply ingrained systems can stall progress—or worse, send mixed signals about what really matters. If the visible markers of leadership stay the same, the perception of change remains weak.

This is not just about hierarchy. It is about influence. Every organization has people who carry more than just expertise—they carry the culture, followership, and credibility that others naturally align with. If these individuals are not actively positioned within transformation efforts, the organization is effectively signaling hesitation, whether intentionally or not.

Unfortunately, staffing for change is often delegated to individual functional leaders—many of whom may not fully grasp the broader ambition or interdependencies involved. When this happens, decisions get made in silos and resistance builds beneath the surface, slowing progress. Difficult as these conversations are, I have seen the best staffing restructurings happen when leadership tackles them collectively, working backward from the desired state.

> **If the visible markers of leadership stay the same, the perception of change remains weak.**

One great consumer products company understood the emotional difficulty of this process and deliberately created space for leaders to step away from their day-to-day pressures before making staffing decisions. Instead of arriving armed with spreadsheets to defend existing structures, leaders spent the first day detaching from reality, walking in the woods, clearing their minds, and eating restorative food. The second day, they were exposed to rare and foreign sports activities, disrupting old thinking patterns. On the third day, after a meditation and breathwork session, they came together to effectively restaff for the future. The shift was subtle but profound: They were solving for what was needed, not for what had already been.

This example illustrates a common pitfall: Even when a company intellectually recognizes the need for change, deeply ingrained systems can stall progress—or worse, send mixed signals about what really matters. If the visible markers of leadership stay the same, the perception of change remains weak.

Respected, influential leaders who could accelerate change are kept in their existing functions—not because they are not capable of leading transformation, but because their presence in legacy roles is seen as too important. The logic is understandable: Stability is comforting, and shifting trusted people can feel like an unnecessary disruption. But the reality is that if transformation is truly the ambition, why are the most credible and respected people not leading it? If their current functions are so well run, should they not have successors ready to step in? And if they don't, what does that say about the organization's ability to scale?

This kind of clarity in staffing decisions is critical, because transformation goes beyond strategies and is about creating a critical mass of those who are able to bring those strategies to life. Leaders must do an honest assessment of their teams:

- Who is suited for the future and ready to adapt?

- Who has the will and skill to succeed in the new environment?

- Who has the will and drive but lacks the necessary skills?

- Who has the skills but lacks the will to change?

- And who has neither?

The last two groups—those who lack both the will and the skill—represent the most significant barriers to change. If left unaddressed, they can drag the process down and slow progress across the organization.

Years ago, I was part of a large-scale transformation, integrating businesses and managing a strategic restructuring of approximately 80,000 people. At the time, Boston Consulting Group (BCG) was our partner, and they introduced a powerful perspective: If we wanted to bring new capabilities to market, rather than repeating what had been done before, at least 30 percent of the organization needed to reflect these new skills. At first, this number felt huge. But when we looked at what was needed to succeed—starting fresh rather than mapping only from existing teams—the 30 percent gap became obvious. In fact, when many companies try to cut back or restructure, it's often easier to mentally remove 50 percent and then staff up again, rather than trying to trim at the edges. The key is ensuring a clear strategic ambition is in place, because staffing should align with where the organization is headed, not where it happens to be today.

While 30 percent is a high number, it is still a minority. And integration is essential for success. Even when the right mix is achieved, one common pitfall remains: integration. Businesses in change often split into two camps: the new hires, who see themselves as the future and assume they know it all, and the incumbents, who resist the shift and reject the new ways of working. At times, one group is in favor; at other times, the other. But neither is correct. The true value lies in integration—in building a shared journey rather than a battle for dominance. Done well and managed by a strong leader, this creates pride, ownership, and mutual learning across all stages of transformation.

Where staffing and human management do indeed require great emotional intelligence both for the individual and for the successful creation of teams, this is not to be mistaken with the exercise of defining what is required. A successful transformation requires leaders to thoroughly assess the organization's history, values, and ingrained workflows while identifying outdated processes that hinder progress.

Transforming an organization is not just about implementing new strategies or technologies; it's about changing the hearts and minds of the people who bring those strategies to life. It's about creating a critical mass of individuals who are willing not just to adapt but to actively embrace the new ways of working, the new mindsets, and the new skills required to thrive in a changing world. And because transformation is never a one-time event, this process must often be repeated at multiple stages of the journey.

CREATING PATHWAYS FOR GROWTH

Staffing is not just about filling roles for the current transformation; it's about curating the right mix of sustained growth and evolution. The same goes for the business as for the people; therefore, staff should always be able to see the value they gain from any assignment, becoming stronger and more attractive resources as a result. In the context of staffing for change, it is crucial to view talent as resources on loan, with the responsibility to make them stronger during their time in the organization. When you borrow resources, you take good care of them and make sure they are not damaged or run down when you hand them over again, just as every employee, ideally, feels responsible for creating value for their business. Without that, there is no business to build on. If people are not given the right challenges, opportunities, and support to grow, their potential is wasted, and so is the organization's investment in them.

The cost of misalignment is high. Leaders who hesitate to make necessary changes often lose twice—first, by holding onto disengaged employees who recognize they no longer belong and, second, by blocking opportunities for others who could drive progress. But the solution is not just about making cuts; it is about ensuring that every individual gains greater value from their role—both extrinsically and intrinsically. Without this, organizations will struggle to attract and retain the talent they need.

A more agile and respectful approach to human resource management ensures that talent contributes at its highest potential while also growing in value. This creates space for existing talent to lean in with pride while making room for new capabilities. When everyone is clear on what they contribute, moving individuals to different functions or stages of the transformation becomes less of a challenge. The goal is not to create a workforce of interchangeable generalists, but to develop a nuanced, honest understanding of each person's skills and how these align with the company's evolving needs. This is a mindset that often thrives in smaller businesses but tends to be forgotten as companies grow and become more siloed. However, there is no longer an excuse for this, as digital tools enable greater access to data, capturing competencies not by filling out sheets but by analyzing peoples' work, calendars, contributions, and impact. This enables a workforce that moves fluidly across the organization, strengthening both the individuals and the business as a whole. When individuals have clear paths for growth and are given the right challenges, they become invested in the company's success. At the same time, they should feel empowered to move on when their skills no longer align with the company's direction.

The key is fostering a culture where talent feels connected to the organization's goals and is open to stepping into new roles, knowing that their growth benefits both the company and their future career path. Too many career conversations become about tenure, expectations, and managed emotions, rather than inviting a conversation about where everyone can contribute most effectively. To achieve this, you must create an environment where employees feel supported in their development, not just expected to adapt. This means showing many different pathways for growth, providing mentorship, and encouraging continuous learning. When individuals see that their efforts contribute to a larger vision and that their skills are valued, they become more willing to embrace change. By prioritizing transparency, feedback, and opportunities for advancement, organizations can transform hesitation into enthusiasm, ensuring that professional growth aligns with both individual aspirations and company success. Because a culture of venturing and openness is also one where each employee stands confidently in their contribution but is also happy to move on to elsewhere if their value is not right for the next phase.

TRANSFORMATION STARTS AT THE TOP

Transformation often does not stall because of bad strategy. It stalls because the desire for change is not strong enough where it matters most. I have encountered great executives, passionate and committed to driving change, with whom backing from majority shareholders or investors did not align, and they had to face the devastating realization that they had been given the illusion of authority but not the power to lead. I've also experienced the opposite, where executives proudly presented their understanding of progress, which fell far short of what those who put the money on the table believed in. Or, even worse, when both owners and executives claim they are aligned but have no intention of change and the unknowing staff tries in vain.

Staffing the board and executive team for the future will not be sufficient if the 30 percent is represented by only a few of the members. The shared ownership of the outcome will make or break a change. Executive expressing buy-in and support will never be enough. You must have the courage to deeply understand the full scope and cost of change, particularly when it involves changing the propositions, shifting business models, or evolving markets.

As an executive, I see myself as the architect of change. I push for innovation, champion new strategies, and take pride in moving businesses forward. But leadership also means recognizing the reality of my own influence. I've seen firsthand how executive teams react when change is on the table. There's typically a mix of responses—worry, excitement, and discreet disengagement. I remember one moment in particular: Two years after a strategy had been signed off by the board, an executive openly admitted, "Ah, now I get it." I give him kudos for the honesty but figuring out how to respond in that moment wasn't easy. It made me reflect on how much time and effort had been lost—time that could have been mobilized more effectively. I imagine you've likely faced similar moments, realizing in hindsight how a strategy could have been communicated or executed differently. How eagerly do we progress versus genuinely check in for understanding and alignment to ensure everyone contributes to progress?

This is also why few businesses transform without a shift in leadership. The rare CEO who drives reinvention within their own tenure stands out precisely because they are the exception. More often, true transformation happens when new leadership steps in—not as a failure of the previous leader, but as a recognition that different moments require different capabilities. I've already mentioned Satya Nadella's shift of Microsoft; there are other known leaders who came in with a clear change mandate for transformational change, such as Paul Polman at Unilever. The much shorter list of exceptions includes Reed Hastings's long leadership and transformation of Netflix, Jeff Bezos's of Amazon, and seemingly also Jensen Huang's journey with Nvidia. Alternatively, having a strong upcoming executive—not the CEO—lead the change is seen a lot. This is a lower-risk approach, which can be a safeguard to not rock the boat too much but also to test the strategy before this person can later take over as CEO, as was seen with Mary Barra at General Motors.

This dependency on an executive sponsor of change is always critical to transformation. I have never seen transformations fully succeed without an executive sponsor who is trusted by both the ownership and the executive team. The leadership required to front such a change goes far beyond the executive remit, relying heavily on the amount of executive air cover provided to those building toward the change. The best change sponsors typically understand both the old and the new, express an extra sense of calm and perspective from having delivered proven results, and are less focused on immediate personal validations. Do you know who these people are in your organization?

As leading change requires new skills, it also requires creating space for them. The very capabilities that once made an executive successful can easily become insufficient, and where skills can be brought in to complement and support, it is just as important for executives to engage themselves in learning with their teams. The best executives don't just set strategy from the top; they stay connected to the intelligence within their teams. One CEO I worked with understood this better than most. He ran a global, industry-leading business, yet he recognized that the expertise fueling the organization was evolving faster than he could track. Rather than relying solely on reports and structured updates, he set up something simple but transformative: a monthly morning session where junior team members would talk with him about his own business. No layers of hierarchy in the room, no filtered messaging, just real conversations. Their leaders took a supporting role, only there to create context and bridge when needed. If the leaders took up too much space, the CEO would deliberately turn back to the junior team, reinforcing the message that he wanted to hear from them. These sessions were rewarding on so many levels, and the CEO was surprised when he realized his teams included anthropologists who were uncovering customer behaviors in ways he had never considered. Often, he found this discussion and two-way mentoring so compelling that he ended up canceling his remaining meetings for the day to continue learning. What separates good leaders from great ones is not just intelligence or experience but a genuine curiosity and willingness to keep learning, challenge assumptions, and listen beyond familiar voices. Because the moment you stop learning, you stop leading.

IDENTIFYING CHANGE MAKERS

Transformational change doesn't just happen at the executive level. Across all the successful organizations I have seen, there are always some passionate change makers often at the CEO-2 level. The most effective change makers combine deep functional expertise with a passion for innovation. These leaders represent energy, drive, and stamina and are not just willing to lead change but capable of inspiring others to do so. Crucially, they can articulate and demonstrate what change looks like in practice and translate ideas into actions. They are curious, seek external insights, and are committed to the organization's success beyond their individual roles. These are not formal jobs but traits of leaders within an organization, and if you have many, you are lucky, but in my experience, most businesses just have a few. And, importantly, change makers are business owners, not change partners.

Leading transformation is rarely a comfortable role. Change makers operate in a space of constant friction—challenging norms, questioning longstanding processes, and pushing for progress. This often places them in a lone position, similar to top executives, but often without the experience to manage this. Success can create tension, even jealousy, in those who are more comfortable with the status quo. And when setbacks occur, they often become the easiest targets for blame. The challenge for these leaders is staying connected—remaining accepted and part of the broader organization and staying close to the pulse of change. An essential part of the success of a change maker is always a close and trusted relationship with one or a few executive sponsors. I have also seen change makers benefit from informal networks both internally or externally, providing essential lifelines and offering perspectives and resilience when resistance builds. Often these roles hold a specific responsibility, a chapter in the transformation journey, and therefore their role is rarely to embed themselves indefinitely but to drive change forward and then pass the baton onto the next change maker.

This is also why change makers are an essential part of transformation, because they demonstrate the fact that change is not something that happens to you, it is something you embody. They set the pace, challenge inertia, and actively shape the future. Mapping and moving change makers strategically ensures that both the organization and these individuals continue to thrive—feeding the business with fresh momentum while keeping their drive for transformation engaged. Like all staffing decisions, this must be done with a clear strategic lens, ensuring placements are made based on business needs rather than sentiment. If left stagnant, even the most effective change makers can lose impact, or worse, become a source of friction rather than progress.

ADDRESSING RESISTANCE TO CHANGE

People are the foundation of transformation. They will carry the organization into its next chapter, making staffing decisions critical and, therefore, transformation is one of the most important levers of success. All too often, businesses lean too heavily on external support. Transformation cannot be outsourced, because lasting change must be built and led from within by those responsible for the company's future.

External expertise can be invaluable, bringing fresh perspectives, surfacing blind spots, and helping leaders carry the burden as they grow themselves. However, the role of external support should be to inform and enable, not to take ownership. Overreliance on external voices creates fragility—organizations risk implementing strategies that lack internal commitment, leaving leaders unprepared to sustain them. Time and again, I have seen change efforts stall the moment external support steps away.

Transformation is not a one-time initiative—it's an ongoing evolution. If you delegate it externally, rather than embedding change capabilities within their teams, then you do not train your organization's change muscles and will find yourself repeatedly bringing in outside help to course-correct. Worse, this cycle erodes trust within the organization.

Outsourcing from the business owners to transformation teams will never create the same engrained change. Lasting change must be led from within by those who will shape and deliver the company's future. Leaders must ensure that teams are enriched by their tenure—supported in their journey, empowered to lead, and fully equipped to move within or outside the business.

The challenge is, of course, that transformation places additional strain on already stretched teams. A common mistake is overloading key people—placing them on multiple initiatives at once and expecting them to contribute at an unsustainable level. When every leader assumes their project is the top priority, but the same individuals are spread thin across four or five high-stakes initiatives, no real shift can occur. Expecting an individual to contribute at 450 percent because each line manager demands to have them at 100 percent leads to burnout, inefficiency, and disengagement. At some point, people stop believing in the change, not because they oppose it but because the way that they are expected to operate within it is impossible. However, when people are planned for as is done with product resources, based on a solid and honest understanding of competencies and utilization, such an engineering mindset can help highlight where resources should flow before the strain on individuals becomes damaging.

Resistance is often mistaken as a rejection of change when, in reality, it is a natural response to uncertainty and misalignment. At the individual level, resistance is often rooted in fear—fear of losing relevance, fear of displacement, or fear of adapting to new expectations. So where you as a leader naturally must acknowledge this by creating space for dialogue, you must manage the conversation toward the ambition and the opportunity to redefine your learning, position, and growth within this change.

At the team level, resistance is more complex. Teams that have established ways of working often struggle when decision-making structures shift, collaboration models evolve, or leadership dynamics change. But with an empowering venturing approach, teams must feel involved and together help channel expertise where it is needed going forward. The best teams are the ones that understand they together support an organization with resources that morph toward where value is best delivered, and where there is space for some within the team to move fast and others to follow. Consistently, they demonstrate progression instead of being locked in the past.

At the organizational level, resistance is deeper and more systemic. People can move faster than teams and teams can move faster than organizations. Structures, policies, and long-standing practices create inertia, and the collective weight of embedded habits can feel almost stuck. This is why staffing for change starts with clarity of ambition, assessment of needs, deployment of individuals, investment in growth, and effective and deliberate management of momentum to pick up the pace.

I worked with a CEO who liked to say, "He or she who has the ability also has the responsibility." However, the real question is whether you are aware of the ability, enabling it and allowing your teams to take responsibility. Everything else is a waste of money and a failure to respect the people entrusted with shaping the company's future.

The most effective staffing for transformation happens when leadership teams take a step back—not just reviewing spreadsheets and structures but thinking from the future back. If the business is serious about transformation, talent allocation must reflect that ambition. This means challenging assumptions about who is needed where, when, and why. It requires making decisions that may not be comfortable in the short term but are necessary for long-term success. Leadership in transformation demands both decisiveness and respect in staffing—ensuring that teams are not only aligned with the company's future but also positioned to succeed within it. It is not just about moving people into roles; it is about managing their workloads with intent, creating the conditions for them to engage with the change rather than endure it, and ensuring they have the support to develop within the transformation rather than burn out under it.

11

ARCHITECTING FOR ACHIEVEMENT

Transformation should hopefully deliver exponential growth but often comfort in the next steps is mistaken for progress. The key lies in recognizing when alignment is premature and when experimentation and divergence are necessary before convergence can occur. Without this awareness, you risk optimizing for short-term efficiencies rather than shaping long-term competitive advantage.

Most leaders naturally have one of three mindsets: visionary, builder, or auditor. While your literal role may hold these perspectives, which one shapes how you approach growth and transformation? Visionaries push boundaries, builders turn ideas into reality, and auditors refine and optimize. All have value, but long-term success demands an awareness of when to protect your natural inclinations and when anchoring in them becomes the biggest risk of all.

I remember the first time I intentionally endorsed a period of structured chaos—a year in which product teams focused solely on strengthening their own growth rather than that of the collective value. The risk of delayed alignment was real, but the gain in product strength proved invaluable. What was essential was that it was conscious and communicated. It was a step in the process, which was needed. In fact, sometimes it is essential to embrace and architect for a degree of messiness. Had the team tried to integrate before products had built strength, the offering would have been too weak. The challenge comes when full businesses operate like this, and the responsibility of bringing the offering together gets put on the customer or those closest to the customer. This is not dissimilar to what we see with some of the technological innovations that stand strong in their own right, but those who have built them don't always hold the responsibility of the integration and usage. Unfortunately, this just means that many great offerings get neglected because they are too hard to use, and all efforts end up wasted. So messiness is a part of transformation, but it must be deliberate and articulated. Because, as leaders, being able to clearly communicate the necessity of discomfort sets your organization up for lasting success.

When teams get disconnected from the ambition or morph in a thousand different directions, a simple but powerful tool I often utilize is drawing a trajectory map—a graph with axes typically representing time and value (in any desired metrics).[1] I place a big powerful star in the top right corner, illustrating the ambition. If the teams don't have one, we create one, applying the thinking shared within visioning brought to their context. I then ask teams to plot all their great initiatives onto the chart toward the star. Once all is added, we try to make a progress trajectory from the start toward the star. A couple of things always occur. The first contributions scatter wide across the base, panning out almost like a fan. The subsequent wave starts to look at the elements already delivered, how these can be built on, and how you can make more decisive prioritization and decisions based on the value these have shown. Last, when you have reached your star at the end and ask the teams to go back and connect the dots with the fewest, yet all relevant points, you see a zigzag path through. This is because naturally not all initiatives will deliver as key a value when looked at it broadly as this, but also value is likely to be accumulated if sequenced right. It is fun to do this with a few different lenses on. For example, have three teams hold the same graph and ambition, with one looking at the journey through the customer experience lens, one through the employee experience lens, and the last through the process lens. When brought together, it will certainly change the sequencing of some of the elements projected.

This highlights an essential truth in architecting for achievement: Different perspectives exist in every organization and knowing when to play which card is critical to orchestrating change. Engineers naturally focus on features and functionality, while marketers look at consumer needs and desires. In times of rapid transformation, these perspectives can create friction. But when leaders blend tactical expertise with visionary thinking, and operational efficiency with customer-centric innovation, they ensure that execution and ambition are seamlessly aligned. The ability to harness these different viewpoints is often what separates companies that execute well from those that merely react.

My team at Google was once helping a massive business transformation. The customer had told us that their main cost and process challenge was customer service; however, from doing this exercise, we found that the lack of information from the operational teams would never position the customer service teams to win, so when we repeated the exercise with the operational teams, we found the real key to unlocking value and margins for the business was, in fact, in data contracting. Think about how much money could have been wasted here. If you were to do that for your business, are there decisions you should be making that are being neglected? Could there be budget reallocations that would unlock greater value across the business, even if they represent a fundamental shift from the previous year?

In architecting for achievement as responsible for strategic business transformation at Google, I have also, along with my talented team, done a similar exercise at industry level. When we looked at the industry movements and started to decode the patterns, it was striking to see that executives typically only chose from a handful of strategic options. Within an industry, the fundamental strategies often boil down to just two to six distinct paths. Understanding these options is not just about competitive awareness; it is about deciding where you seek to shape an industry and where you position yourself to actively ride the coattails of others.

Pioneers create new value pools, shift ecosystems, and challenge existing structures. Market reapers optimize within established models, benefiting from shifts driven by others. Both can be very profitable, but remember that the pioneers often get to define the rules of engagement—so we need to be sure there is enough growth within the followers if we choose to play here. Take banking: The industry is already evolving, yet large institutions hesitate. Smaller players disrupt by showing customers different forms of engagement, some by taking a greater role in managing their economy. The assets these banks hold—vast amounts of customer data, behavioral insights, and lifecycle spending information—are some of the most powerful tools available to them. Yet they sit on it. They know more about their customers than anyone else, but how are they using that information and building a platform to become undisputable based on the volume of insights they build?

Leadership is about seeing the storm coming and steering the ship before anyone else does.

Leadership is about seeing the storm coming and steering the ship before anyone else does. Assets alone don't guarantee leadership; it's the strategic application of those assets that defines success.

Whether you are shaping an industry or optimizing within one, you must stay vigilant—listening for internal and external signals, understanding when to push forward, when to pause, and when to course-correct. Architecting for achievement requires both bold moves and the humility to pivot when new dynamics emerge. The same mindset of knowing when to shape and when to optimize applies at every level of decision-making, from industry positioning down to individual business priorities.

DECISIVE PRIORITIZATION

Success in a rapidly evolving landscape isn't about limiting innovation but about channeling energy, capital, and strategic attention toward the most impactful opportunities, ensuring that the right bets are placed at the right time to drive meaningful progress. No one has unlimited resources, and fortunately so. Constraints sharpen prioritization. The ability to prioritize effectively, interpret data wisely, and make decisive trade-offs separates those who execute transformation from those who merely track its progress. Not only this, but studies also show that leaders who make swift, clear decisions are perceived as more competent and trustworthy.[2]

Businesses that struggle with prioritization often fall into one of two traps—either spreading resources too thin by chasing every opportunity without depth or focusing solely on optimizing the current model while overlooking critical shifts in the landscape. The real challenge lies in balancing ambition with execution—ensuring that new ideas have the space to emerge while staying firmly connected to the operational demands of sustaining profitability and growth. True optimization happens when leaders integrate new thinking seamlessly into the business, driving both immediate impact and long-term adaptability.

Companies that thrive in exponential environments have mastered the art of sequencing, knowing which ideas to pursue aggressively, which to develop quietly in the background, and which to deliberately pause until the ecosystem is ready. This is where one of the old tools—desirable, feasible, and viable—becomes more than a theoretical framework; it becomes a discipline of constantly assessing: What is ready to be scaled today? What needs further investment before it can create exponential returns? What is currently blocking or diluting our highest-potential initiatives?

Many businesses fail simply because they don't commit deeply enough to the few things that will truly change their trajectory. The most successful industry disruptors do not hedge their bets evenly across every possibility—they make decisive choices about where to place strategic weight. As explored earlier, businesses that set up small innovation teams with the intent of innovations building new, separate revenue streams or intrapreneurship that will drive change across a wider business often fail when core performance metrics remain tied to existing revenue streams. Then the leader has not enabled the business and steered toward real change. This is where prioritization becomes a test of leadership clarity. An idea may be desirable and feasible, but what would it take for it to become viable? Think about it:

- Desirable: Does this solve a real problem for customers, employees, or the market?

- Feasible: Do you have the capabilities, resources, and technology to execute it effectively?

- Viable: Will this create long-term value and align with financial and strategic goals?

Organizations frequently drift into imbalances, often under the illusion of sound decision-making. This is due not to negligence but rather to the gravitational pull of leadership biases, incentive structures, and deeply embedded organizational habits.

Prioritization often fails when excitement takes over and leaders rush to stake a claim in what appears to be the future without laying the operational groundwork to scale. So instead of running heedlessly with it, a good venturing leader would instead ask: What would it take for this to succeed at scale? What needs to change structurally to make this a sustainable advantage? The operational blind spot is common in execution-heavy organizations, where feasibility dominates decision-making. The default assumption? If it can be built, it should be built. Engineering-driven teams, for instance, prioritize technical excellence but often overlook whether the market actually needs what they are optimizing. This is why many organizations produce flawless products that fail commercially. This trap is particularly dangerous because it feels like progress—teams deliver on their road maps, efficiency improves, and internal goals are met. But none of it matters if customers are indifferent. The fix is not about slowing execution but about forcing customer impact into the conversation early and often. Leaders must regularly challenge teams: Who needs this? How do we know? What happens if we don't build it?

The financial tunnel vision is the most difficult to detect because it aligns with traditional measures of business success—profitability, cost control, and operational efficiency. It tends to surface in legacy organizations and during downturns, when the instinct is to optimize for financial stability over strategic expansion. The logic is straightforward: cut nonessential costs, refine core processes, and double down on what is already working. But viability without desirability and feasibility leads to stagnation. Companies that focus too much on financial optimization risk eroding their competitive edge, prioritizing immediate gains while missing the underlying shifts happening in consumer behavior and industry dynamics. If financial performance becomes the sole decision-making lens, the business has already lost sight of its future. The way out? Reframe discussions around the cost of inaction. What market opportunities are quietly being lost while focus remains on efficiency? What is the future state of the company in this context?

THE RIPPLE EFFECT OF CHANGE

Prioritization is essential, but transformation never happens in isolation and too often efforts focus on individual components—new technologies, restructuring, market shifts—without considering how they interact. This narrow focus risks creating misalignment, wasted effort, and unintended bottlenecks. The real challenge is not just optimizing individual elements but also ensuring they work together. True transformation requires systems thinking—understanding how changes in one area affect the whole. Just as when we looked at the organization as a nervous system, when one part shifts, signals ripple throughout the business. Similarly, here it is useful to see it as a web of nerve endings radiating from a central command. Tug on one thread, and the entire structure responds.

Many companies have spent huge efforts in process mining to uncover inefficiencies, but without a bigger-picture perspective, even well-optimized processes can create unintended consequences elsewhere. Carrefour, a leading French retailer, on the other hand, was among the first to market with generative AI and made headlines for their innovation. However, the real success came from their internal adjustments, not just the technology. The media coverage spoke about shelf sell-out data and a contribution toward a 12 percent increase in consumer satisfaction, but what the AI insights revealed was, in fact, where decision-making was too slow, exposing the need for structural change, which a decisive leader acted on and made the headlines. They simplified decision-making structures, giving store managers greater autonomy. It will be the 30 percent increase in decision-making speed, and the lower operational costs, that will keep delivering for them across more categories, not just the tech deployment.

Shifting to a more data-driven culture will always require overcoming resistance to new ways of working and often investing in training. Decentralizing decision-making as in this case also introduces challenges in maintaining consistency across different stores and regions. However, by continuously celebrating successes across different business areas, they have been able to continue to fuel momentum and success, demonstrating that adapting to interdependencies increases collective value.

This change was structured as it unfolded with the support of AI and strong leadership, but I have also seen how creating broader views can successfully create an environment for the right change conversations. I have more than once been part of managing interdependencies through mapping the entire customer journey with cross-functional teams.

Following the user or the customer through their step-by-step interactions with a business can be very valuable, making it visible, large for all to see, and having multiple teams contribute, showing where they interact. Teams from research and development, marketing, product, finance, and manufacturing—all working together—created sight of bottlenecks as well as interdependencies. A customer journey view allows leaders to visualize whether initiatives have the necessary organizational support. Imagine that early-stage teams are enthusiastic about a new proposition, but by the time it reaches manufacturing, the necessary resources or commitment is missing. Or following a product through the user journey only to find that the customer will be disappointed in post-sales servicing. Beyond just mapping interactions, I have seen this approach be used to evaluate costs at various stages, shape a customer profitability view, assess customer satisfaction touchpoints, and provide an early warning system for overburdened functions. Of course, building this through interconnected data sources and enabling your AI to suggest improvements is where you should be going, but in the process never underestimate the change impact of having people build their own prioritization views. If you did this for your business, would there be any surprises? And by sharing, would it help your organization not just architect together but also change together, lift together, and succeed together?

Understanding interdependencies is only valuable if businesses align this to measuring the right things. Too often, KPIs reinforce silos rather than optimizing the system as a whole. The next step is reassessing performance metrics—ensuring that what gets measured drives alignment, not friction. Leaders who integrate KPI management into their transformation efforts create organizations that aren't just moving but are moving in the right direction.

STEERING TRANSFORMATION

Managing businesses has always demanded an ownership of outcomes and results, which often gets simplified into managing performance. The real question, though, is what to measure and how to ensure a balance between appropriate leading indicators and the results.

Netflix's evolution offers a clear example of intentional KPI management. Their shift from DVD rentals to streaming wasn't just about technology—it was about knowing which metrics to flex and when. As the business transitioned, they moved from prioritizing DVD delivery efficiency to streaming engagement, proactively evolving their KPIs to match the realities of their transformation. This ability to adjust measurement systems in lockstep with strategic direction is what separates agile companies from those stuck in legacy thinking.

Too often, companies fail because they hold onto too many KPIs or overlook interdependencies between them. It is not inherently wrong to have conflicting KPIs—in fact, they can be useful in highlighting trade-offs. But delegating alignment and failing to create feedback loops that help teams interpret results in misalignment, wasted energy, and conflicting priorities at different levels of the organization. Without clear communication, leaders risk teams either resisting change or pulling in opposite directions. Many companies make the mistake of setting surgical priorities without explaining why they matter. Consider the corporate rush to invest in AI. For many, it was not about immediate profitability—it was about securing a presence in the market and embedding learning within the business. Yet, without clear articulation, employees often push back, questioning the relevance of their work. The rapid adoption of AI also requires businesses to reassess traditional KPIs to accurately reflect productivity and efficiency shifts, as seen in Walmart's use of AI-driven demand forecasting, which reduced stockouts by 30 percent through real-time adjustments based on weather patterns and local events, giving them a powerful leading indicator of performance, which again enabled them to win ahead of their industry.[3] This is an example of what in the early days was mostly done through social listening, ensuring that performance metrics reflected external realities, not just internal benchmarks. Goals set for internal performance rarely change with the context and resources fast enough and therefore result in skepticism. The power is in transforming KPI management from a rigid reporting exercise into a proactive decision-making tool supported by clear communication. Organizations that regularly reassess their KPIs—at least quarterly, or even monthly in fast-moving industries—are better positioned to anticipate change rather than react to it.[4]

Many businesses have relied on structured transformation methods such as Lean Optimization, Six Sigma, Quality Management, and Process

Reengineering—approaches designed for stability and predictability. These methods improve efficiency and reduce waste, but they struggle to accommodate the kind of rapid shifts that market-driven transformations demand. As leaders, we therefore need to challenge rigid playbooks and instead focus on adaptability, integrating external signals into decision-making rather than relying solely on internal efficiency metrics. We need to ensure that our KPIs evolve with business ambition rather than reinforcing outdated processes. We need to recognize when speed is more critical than precision, particularly in new market opportunities. And specifically, many need to reflect on whether we are asking middle management the right questions, asking them for trends and their underlying patterns, initiatives with scaling potential, cross-organizational connections, and any risks instead.

Architecting for achievement means ensuring that KPIs serve the business, not the other way around. It requires leaders to, beyond any insightful data, foster the human capacity for judgment to steer transformations with conviction, responsibility, and flexibility.

Architecting for achievement means ensuring that KPIs serve the business, not the other way around.

Architecting for achievement means understanding that transformation is an evolving journey. Leaders must constantly assess the pace of change and create a rhythm that keeps the organization moving forward while providing comfort in times of uncertainty. Ultimately, transformation is about building momentum through a rhythm of progress, ensuring that teams align around a common ambition while maintaining the autonomy to drive change within their own spheres. We as leaders must ensure that all teams are set up to move in the same direction, capable and empowered to contribute and innovate in support of the organization's long-term success.

Part III Reflections to Motivate Action: Are You Steering as You Lead in Motion?

Leadership in motion is meeting change with open eyes, expansive breath, and steady hands—moving with clarity, so others feel ready to step forward with you.

- *Deliberate support for change allies:* How intentionally are you identifying and supporting both fast movers and fast followers for your change—creating the partnerships and conditions that lift each other and carry it further together?

- *Talent aligned to future needs:* Is your business staffed for the past or the future—and are you consistently signaling what's desired through both the placement and the reward of people and how you communicate it?

- *Metrics that matter:* How clearly do your metrics reinforce the behaviors and outcomes you want more of—and how are you evolving what you track, encourage, and reward to reflect where the business needs to go?

....

PART IV

EMBODYING

True transformation happens from within—it's not about standing still, but about having the spine to stand strong while adapting with agility and creating followership through embodied conviction.

12

EMBODYING TRANSFORMATIONAL LEADERSHIP

The strongest leaders are not those who simply react to change, or those who disengage, but those who see beyond the immediate pressures and move with deliberate intent—leaders who create space for teams to feel safe to contribute within, embrace new possibilities while safeguarding what matters most, and move fast without losing direction. The challenge is not just about implementing new technologies; it is about ensuring you align with what the business wins within the future ecosystem, thereby reinforcing your identity and strategic position rather than diluting it. However, many leaders still remain locked in a pattern of forceful execution, pushing initiatives forward, solving for the immediate, and ensuring targets are met.

Often, this happens when speed is prioritized over intention—intention that shapes the long-term trajectory of the business. This is not about having the right answers; it is about knowing which questions matter, recognizing the patterns that shape decisions, and having the conviction to act even in uncertainty. It creates advantages in an evolving business landscape, clarity in the midst of competing priorities, and a greater invitation to deploy yourself as a leader who can navigate these shifts.

This is where leadership strength is truly tested. Not in how tightly you hold on, but in how wisely you let go.

THE STRENGTH OF LETTING GO

I was once at a CEO retirement reception. As I greeted the retiring CEO, another newly appointed CEO from a different company walked up. The retiring CEO turned to the new leader and remarked, "Yes, it is my turn now, but you know that your board has already commenced discussing when and with whom they will replace you." They shared a cordial smile and a light laugh, yet both understood that the comment was far from mere jest. A CEO's role is to accomplish a mission, and when that mission is either achieved, no longer aligns with the organization's needs, or goes off-course, a change becomes necessary. Yet the leaders who transition most successfully are those who have already done the internal work—who understand their own trajectory and can step aside with clarity rather than fear. The ability to move on without uncertainty stems not from external validation but from a deep understanding of your own identity and from there, your role and contribution.

I have seen CEOs who, having reached their objectives faster than expected, chose to step aside—even if it meant the organization would exclaim, "But hey, you just joined!" This is certainly not a call for a hasty personnel change; rather, it's a recognition that the essence of leadership lies in intent and achievement, not in titles. While experience is invaluable, there comes a moment when the accumulated wisdom has fulfilled its role, and a graceful transition becomes the best way to honor both past contributions and future potential.

In fact, one of the hardest—and least discussed—elements of leadership is knowing when to let go. And transformation is letting go to make way for what is next. While easiest illustrated with role changes, this happens all the time on a smaller scale when stepping away from initiatives that do not serve anymore. Some of the hardest decisions involve closing projects that once held great promise but no longer serve the business. Leaders often pour time, energy, and resources into initiatives that, despite their initial potential, do not yield the expected results. Some businesses have a tendency of overentertaining the discussion of whether to do or not to do and potentially starve projects so they never get off the ground, whereas many others kill projects by slowly showing disbelief without fully stepping away. Those who do it best ensure full support once an initiative is supported, indicate a willingness to reopen the conversation if new data arises from within the project or outside, and make responsible decisions to close or move learnings to where they can help lift another part of the venture.

However, for most, the emotional investment makes it too tempting to persist, to try one more adjustment, one more push. But what makes this process truly difficult is not just the external factors—the investment of time, resources, and credibility—but, even more, the internal struggle of detaching from an identity tied to past success. When identity is too closely tied to external achievements, stepping away feels like a loss rather than a strategic choice. Leadership is often deeply tied to identity and legacy, which is why if leaders seek validation solely through performance achievements, they place the responsibility for their self-worth on external outcomes. This creates a fragile foundation, one in which success is measured by control rather than by momentum and in which stepping back can feel like diminishing your own relevance.

I have seen many talented individuals, driven by external recognition, tirelessly working toward achievements that may never come. I, too, have been there—chasing validation only to find that it felt hollow when it arrived. This realization helped me understand that the real value of leadership has nothing to do with recognition and everything to do with enabling others and building from within.

Time and again, my strategy teams and I have worked with executives struggling to make bold business decisions—only to uncover that, beneath it all, they are still following a much more personal drive. Perhaps it is the unspoken approval of a parent—a parent who is not part of the company. This personal drive will never be recognized in the way they hope. Yet this unresolved need for validation silently shapes their priorities, influencing risk tolerance, strategic choices, and even leadership style. The real challenge is not just in making the right business decisions but in freeing yourself from invisible constraints.

I've found that the best leaders find different paths to pride—paths that clear their focus, shift their attention to what truly matters, and allow them to lead with authenticity. Through my own experience, I've learned that those who have done the inner work and who have clarity on their own evolution navigate these transitions, not with reluctance, but with a sense of forward movement. True leadership, I've come to recognize, isn't about proving worth through persistence. It's about knowing when persistence is no longer the best use of my energy.

A striking yet rare example of this comes from Denmark, where Queen Margrethe II handed down the crown of Denmark. While this may seem like a nonsense fairytale, consider the responsibility you would feel as the world's longest-reigning royal, greatly loved by your people, in possession of respect and followership far exceeding what most would expect in today's day in age. Imagine also that you do not have a choice of who continues the reign after you (her son, more jovial, very likable, but not at all with the same level of experience and grounding). Traditionally, most monarchs choose to continue to serve in their roles until they die, as opposed to abdicating the throne while still alive. However, Margrethe II recognized that true leadership is not just staying the course but also setting up for future success—and doing so from a place of confidence, not attachment. She understood that the ability to step aside is liberating when one has cultivated the self-awareness and inner clarity to do so with certainty and confidence. She spent all her working time ensuring that everyone was set up to succeed after her tenure, while giving space for those who followed to create their own mark and legacy.

Cultivating responsible and accountable clarity with respect to ourselves is both liberating and particularly relevant in today's business world, where both leadership transitions and managing priorities and investments are becoming more complex. Just as acknowledging an inevitable ascension, knowing when to step away from projects that no longer serve builds trust with teams that their efforts will not be wasted. It is a sign of both strategic clarity and personal leadership strength.

Mobius Executive Leadership, also heavily endorsed and leveraged by executive development and headhunting company Egon Zehnder, has since 2005 studied leadership mastery as a balance between structure and emergence—knowing when to apply existing knowledge and when to surrender to new insights. But this balance is only possible when a leader has a strong internal foundation. Without clarity about their own ability to navigate change, leaders either hold on too long or let go too soon, not because of strategy but because of uncertainty within themselves.[1] As we have seen from most of the stories in this book, true leadership is not about rigid control but about cultivating the inner clarity to stand firm while adapting. If transformation requires letting go, then movement—both mental and strategic—is essential. This is not about rigid control, or a blind surrender to what happens around you, but about cultivating a deep self-awareness that enables you to remain steady while navigating change proactively.

DEVELOPING SELF-AWARENESS

Good leaders know that leadership is not just about knowing the business—that is the easy part, and it can be calculated. It is about knowing yourself, your values, and how your experiences shape the decisions you make. Not self-awareness to the point of overthinking or emotional exhaustion, but to the level where you remain deeply connected to personal values and worth. Because when teams follow a strategy, they follow the leader. When investors invest, they invest in leadership. And leadership demands clarity, not just in action but in being.

Leading Through: Activating the Soul, Heart, and Mind of Leadership, authored by former Harvard Business School dean Kim B. Clark and his children, Jonathan R. Clark and Erin E. Clark, reinforces the power of leading through connection rather than authority.[2] Their research highlights the value unlocked through increased initiative and contributions, demonstrating that impactful leadership arises not from exerting power over others but from leading through them.

In 2007, Otto Scharmer introduced *Theory U: Leading from the Future as It Emerges*, a framework addressing profound transformations in both organizations and individuals.[3] Building on nearly two decades of research in action learning, systems thinking, and organizational learning, Scharmer's *Theory U* guides leaders through a process of releasing outdated patterns, sensing emerging possibilities, and taking action from a place of deeper awareness. This methodology emphasizes developing seven essential leadership capacities to create futures that would not otherwise be possible.[4]

As seen with visioning and expanding, this work is underpinned by the importance of starting with openness. Here, specifically, that means an *open mind*, in which you must suspend judgment, challenge assumptions, and move beyond automatic responses to see opportunities with new clarity. The next stage involves cultivating an *open heart*, which is about deeply observing and understanding the system, connecting with stakeholders, and developing empathy to sense what is truly needed. The stage where a business would also think expansively, consider partners, and empower wider to gain greatest contribution. Finally, at the base of the U, an *open will*—the moment where leaders let go of rigid control and preconceived strategies and connect with a moment of profound reflection—almost stillness—allowing new possibilities to emerge from the process. In this sense, will is not about imposing a fixed plan but about being present enough to move with what is unfolding.

As the upward part of the U begins, leaders test ideas and solutions and cocreate toward a scaling transformation. The value of this upward journey lies in moving from insight to innovation—bringing fresh solutions into reality, grounded in collective input and emerging from a deeper understanding. *Theory U* also encourages leaders to unlearn outdated approaches, tap into the collective intelligence of their teams, and codevelop strategies that are adaptive, sustainable, and aligned with emerging realities.

The ability to make decisions not from habit or inherited assumptions, but from full presence, conviction, and a deeper sensing of what is needed. Transformation is often reduced to an exercise in execution—applying familiar strategies to new challenges—yet true impact comes from creating space to recognize what genuinely shifts the system. The real work lies in disrupting ingrained patterns, challenging your own mental models, and accessing the deeper currents shaping the organization.

An open heart is what shifts an ego-system into an ecosystem, moving beyond self-centered perspectives to recognize the interconnectedness of teams, businesses, and industries. And when we as leaders understand how to engage with change not as individual decision-makers but as part of a larger field of intelligence, we unlock a shared capacity for adaptation, innovation, and resilience.

> **An open heart is what shifts an ego-system into an ecosystem.**

By embracing this process, leaders move beyond the illusion of control and into a state of generative action where decisions not only are made but emerge from a clearer, deeper understanding of what is possible. It is in this state that transformation moves beyond structured plans, opens for sensing and contributions, and cultivates the conditions for shared success.

Despite the brain's desire to repeat old patterns, neuroplasticity shows that new pathways can emerge through conscious effort. Research on neural remapping demonstrates that the brain can reorganize itself even when existing pathways are disrupted, forming new connections.[5] Similarly, studies on learning and adaptation show that when needed, areas of the brain can expand through deliberate practice, reflection, and exposure to new stimuli.[6] The brain, just as your business, is not a static system—it adapts, rewires, and evolves when actively engaged in change. But you need to actively design and drive it.

Interestingly, the ability to both hold an open heart and sense your own will—as emphasized in *Theory U*—are not purely cognitive exercises; they require physical embodiment. Just as forming new neural pathways demands repeated, intentional action, the deep transformation of leadership is not achieved through abstract reflection alone. It must be lived. The body and mind are not separate in how they process change—you must not only conceptualize change but physically step into new ways of being.

Building on these principles, I have found that transformation efforts often fail when leaders attempt to move from the present to a vision captured in documents without fully understanding the impact on their own identity. Many leaders are busy doing the work, driving, pushing, and doing what it takes, but when the business moves to a state where the former leaders find themselves disassociated from it, the business and expectations now start leading them rather than the other way around. They become figures rather than leaders—individuals who fill a role but do not generate followership. Unlike traditional leadership models that emphasize preset goals, true transformation moves from theoretical to embodied when leaders fully engage in the process of sensing and presencing, allowing both identity and strategy to shape within them, before they are then ready to step in with conviction and without fear.

This is why true transformation is often only solidified when leaders not only see new possibilities but physically experience themselves acting differently within them. It is in this embodiment—where intellectual realization translates into lived action—that leaders shift from theoretical change to a presence others can follow.

BECOMING A STABILIZING FORCE

Large shifts—whether in markets, organizations, or industries—always show small signals first. But sensing is not just about observation; it is about perception—and perception is shaped as much by our internal state as by external stimuli. Grounding provides the stability to notice small shifts without being overwhelmed by them and therefore, is what makes true sensing possible. Some find grounding in values, some in faith, and some in purpose. True leadership is not just about what anchors you but how you embody it.

A leader who is mentally scattered or emotionally unsettled will struggle to distinguish weak signals from noise, often reacting to surface-level trends rather than sensing deeper shifts. Many leaders believe they are grounded until the ground shifts beneath them. When faced with uncertainty, some grip tighter, clinging to what they know, hoping for certainty that will never come. Others search for external solutions, looking to others for answers, or ducking to avoid being confronted with the unknown.

The same applies to businesses—those that neglect to pause, reassess, and recalibrate risk missing the very shifts that will determine their future success. In the same way that grounding is not about standing still or appearing calm or in control, establishing the needed presence requires understanding yourself and from there accessing the full range of your own inner resources. Carl Jung posited that true growth comes from acknowledging all aspects of ourselves, including the parts we have left hidden.[7] Too often, leaders push forward by strengthening what they already know. But transformation, both personal and organizational, doesn't come from deepening the known—it comes from expanding into the unknown.

Being grounded is not a passive state but an active discipline—one that sharpens perception, strengthens decision-making, and enables leaders to act with mental clarity and conviction and operate from a place of presence. This heightened awareness is in fact active stillness. In sports, this is called being "ready"—you are grounded, checked in with yourself, fully present, engaged, and ready to move. This is no different in business. Leaders who are grounded in themselves create space for deeper perception, allowing them to detach from external noise and tune in to what actually matters. Likely all leaders will have acknowledged the need for reflection and introspection, but the mind alone does not hold all the answers. Just like thinking through a challenge is different from experiencing it, true presence is not a mental exercise, it is an embodied state.

Research suggests that between 60 percent and 93 percent of communication is nonverbal. Albert Mehrabian's studies in 1971 highlighted the significant impact of nonverbal cues in conveying emotions and attitudes.[8] Similarly, Judee Burgoon, Laura Guerrero, and Kory Floyd's 2016 work underscores the importance of nonverbal signals in human interactions.[9] These subtle physiological signals—such as shifts in posture, breath, or muscle tension—are often the first indicators of a change in the environment. Research shows that the gut and heart contain their own neural networks, processing information faster than the conscious mind. This is why leaders often describe a "gut feeling" about something long before data confirms it. Sensing, then, is not purely intellectual—it is deeply physical. The nervous system constantly scans for patterns, detecting inconsistencies, risks, and emerging opportunities at a subconscious level. When you are attuned to your own bodily responses, you gain access to a more intuitive layer of decision-making—one that integrates logic with embodied awareness.

But modern leadership often works against this natural intelligence. Leadership decisions are frequently made in a state of urgency, engaging the sympathetic nervous system (fight-or-flight response), which prioritizes immediate action over deeper perception. While this can be effective in crisis moments, it is not a sustainable mode for transformation. Becoming truly alert is not about scanning for threats; it is about learning to hold complexity without being consumed by it. True leadership, especially in times of change, requires the ability to access the parasympathetic system, the state in which deep perception, complex thinking, and long-term strategy become possible. This is about holding a state of dynamic equilibrium, where you remain present and attuned to sense beyond the immediate, access a broader field of intelligence, make sharp decisions from clarity rather than impulse, and make moments of transitions defining rather than moments of release. The most effective leaders ensure that decisions are not only responsive but directional, shaping the future rather than chasing it.

Active stillness is not inaction; it enables you to sense movement before it becomes obvious and to remain centered while others are thrown off course. We have all observed the contrast between someone who sits "actively still" in a meeting—listening attentively, owning their position but clearly creating space for others to speak and contribute—and the others who merely occupy the room, or, even worse, those who take up all the air in the room, spreading black clouds around them. They may not be aware of what they're doing, but you feel it. One amplifies awareness; the other narrows it. One fosters contribution; the other diminishes it. Leaders who embody active stillness invite change because they create an environment where others feel safe to share perspectives, knowing that they will not be overburdened by the leader's own fears or uncertainties. True transformation is not just a shift in strategy; it is an embodied shift in how leaders hold themselves within uncertainty. Embodying transformation harmonizes the intellect with intuition, the mind with the body, to create a future that is both strategically sound and deeply resonant.

Those who are unwavering in decision-making are those who are able to control the full spectrum of thinking, spanning logic, intuition, creativity, motivation, and so on, and deploy them effectively. All modes are possible and available to add; however, as executives have often overtrained certain ways of thinking, they neglect the power of thinking. In fact, only 4 percent of respondents in an MIT Sloan study showed they had an understanding of their brain-body connection in thinking.[10]

The distinction lies not in intelligence or skill but in presence. True transformation isn't just understood—it's lived. Leadership requires the ability to integrate rational analysis with the ability to sense, adapt, and act with alignment rather than reaction. The more one is able to sense, the greater the need for structure to effectively deploy insights will be, and equally in reverse, the greater the intellectual complexity, the more important embodied awareness becomes. A present leader is a grounded leader, and grounded leaders move differently. A grounded state of composure allows us as leaders to respond thoughtfully, even under pressure, enhancing both our resilience and the quality of decision-making. It is about deliberate responsiveness and the discipline to balance reflection with decisive action. Leaders who cultivate this become a stabilizing force, not by demanding authority, but by embodying presence—creating the conditions for others to engage, contribute, and navigate uncertainty with confidence. Conversely, we have all seen talented, hardworking individuals who still require constant direction, unable to navigate uncertainty without reassurance. Well-meaning leaders may try to solve this by offering more context or information, but true self-sufficiency rarely comes from external input alone—it comes from developing the internal stability to move forward without uncertainty. So, when leaders embody such presence, consistently, they don't just make better decisions themselves—they create an environment where others learn to do the same.

True leadership is not declared; it is felt. It is seen in how a leader remains grounded, holds space, senses movement, and moves with clarity—not as a reaction to change, but as an active force in shaping it. This is how to lead with conviction, inspire authentic followership, and navigate change with both clarity and courage.

STRENGTHENING YOUR CAPACITY TO LEAD

Out there exists ample literature and content on more efficient routines, sharper decision-making frameworks, or improved time-management strategies. Yet it has been shown time and time again that the real challenge lies not just in building new habits but in unlocking the habitual patterns that limit growth in the first place. Change in organizations requires structural shifts, and changing ourselves demands the same—a deep internal reconfiguration, not just an overlay of new techniques.

Many leaders already integrate physical training into their routines—gym workouts, ice baths, endurance races—all in the name of building stamina, resilience, and stress resilience. But here is a paradox at play: If all physical effort is directed toward output—competing, pushing limits, enduring more—then it may, in fact, reinforce the very patterns that make internal grounding harder to access. I have seen many leaders who excel at pushing through but struggle to step back, sense, and shift when needed. A mind wired for constant performance struggles to engage in true presence, as high-intensity endurance training increases cortisol levels and sustains a fight-or-flight response in the body, potentially reinforcing habitual stress patterns rather than counterbalancing them.[11] Leaders who train only for stamina risk sharpening their ability to persist at the expense of their capacity to sense, adjust, and move with clarity.

On the other side of the spectrum, there is the pursuit of inner stillness—yoga, meditation, breathwork, and so on—all aimed at cultivating awareness, reducing stress, and quieting the mind. These practices can be powerful tools for clarity, creating the space and conditioning the brain needs for deeper insight and emotional regulation.[12] From experience, I have seen the immense value these practices can bring when truly integrated into leadership. However, there is also a risk in treating them as an escape rather than an integration. Some leaders spend hours in deep reflection but never translate it into action. If these practices serve only as a temporary reset—something left behind on the yoga mat or in a quiet room, rather than carried into daily leadership—it can create a divide between awareness and action. True self-regulation is not just about finding moments of calm in a busy schedule; it is about bringing that calm into motion, into decision-making, and into leadership itself.

A few activities naturally manage to bring these two together, such as some martial arts, equestrian sports, rock climbing, free diving, rowing, sailing, parkour, competitive dancing, surfing, and so on. I am sure more could be listed, but in fact, it is more about the mindset with which one engages that determines the value.

Many people also attempt to reconnect through activities that feel like a relief from responsibilities—going out with friends, having a glass of wine or a beer, scrolling through entertainment, or otherwise seeking distraction. These moments of pause are of course natural, but it is a common misunderstanding to think that they help us reconnect with ourselves. Instead, I've realized that training the brain to seek external stimulation as a coping mechanism that reinforces the habit of avoidance rather than building the capacity to process and integrate challenges. If our only way to disconnect from pressure is through escape, then our ability to remain present within challenge also remains untrained.

At the same time, I have seen how true connection—genuine, engaged interaction with others—can be a powerful force in leadership. Engaging in social interactions is not just about relaxation; it actively strengthens emotional regulation, sharpens perspective, and reinforces resilience. Research on social intelligence highlights that strong interpersonal connections enhance a leader's ability to remain composed and adaptable in high-pressure situations.[13] Similarly, time spent in nature has been shown to reduce stress, improve cognitive function, and enhance overall well-being.[14] I believe that stepping outside the constant stream of structured thinking—whether through meaningful conversations, nature, or shared experiences—provides essential recalibration. In fact, exposure to natural environments has a direct impact on attention restoration and decision-making, allowing leaders to process complexity with greater clarity.

Training for embodied leadership does not mean choosing between endurance and recovery or forcing social interactions after a long day at work. It means balancing with intentionality. Just as an athlete must know when to push and when to recover, a leader must know when to cultivate stillness, when to listen rather than act, and when to expand awareness rather than tighten control. Neither leadership nor life is about surviving life until the next break—they are about learning to move through it with strength, clarity, and intention. In my experience, the leaders who navigate change most effectively are those who actively balance these types of activities, with an astute awareness of what they need to develop their leadership at any given time, not as an escape but as a tool in grounding themselves. It is the ability to understand what each does for you that matters. It is like listening to a piece of music: While the beat keeps you grounded, the melody lifts you to new levels. Leaders who cultivate this ability are able to build foundations that help others rise, not just stay within the constraints of tasks or timelines. Younger talents, in particular, have a unique opportunity—not only to start with this mindset but to role-model it, rather than emulate outdated habits that may still linger above them.

Expansion without stability leads to fragility. Leaders who fixate on external shifts without anchoring in something deeper become reactive, chasing and creating busyness and mistaking action for progress. This is the fundamental difference between surviving and thriving. When grounding activities serve only as an outlet to recover from exhaustion, they reinforce a cycle of depletion rather than strengthening the capacity to hold presence. Thriving leaders do not engage in these moments merely to tolerate the next wave of demands; they use them to sharpen their ability to engage with what matters. Challenging our bodies and minds, enjoying a drink, unwinding with some friends, or taking a step back are all fine, but what really matters is whether these moments serve as a way to rewire yourself and return stronger, or simply delay the inevitable engagement with the real challenges at hand.

> Expansion without stability leads to fragility. Leaders who fixate on external shifts without anchoring in something deeper become reactive, chasing and creating busyness and mistaking action for progress.

Leadership presence is not static; it is practiced. And just like any other form of training, the key is repetition. Learning to pause, tune in, and sense before reacting is not a one-time shift; it is a muscle that strengthens with use. The critical factor is not the activity itself but how it is approached: Are you using training, whether physical or mental, to deepen your capacity to lead? Or are you simply compartmentalizing effort, leaving clarity on the course, resilience in the gym, and presence on the meditation mat?

While stoic philosophy has for centuries emphasized that true control comes from the ability to master your own response, modern interpretations often misrepresent this as detachment from influencing more widely. In reality, stoicism champions intentional leadership where clarity of thought and deliberate response create the internal alignment necessary to move decisively, stand firm under pressure, and engage with the unknown without losing direction. True leadership training is not about disconnecting from the world to find balance; it is about integrating what is gained back into everyday decisions, challenges, and interactions. Research shows that learning experienced through the body—whether through action, practice, or physical engagement—creates stronger neural connections and longer retention compared to passive intellectual processing.[15] Lessons that are lived are understood. My experience shows that leaders who truly thrive are those who integrate their practices into how they show up—they train the skill in their lives, apply it in leadership, and live it in their decisions, reinforcing and strengthening their capacity over time. This happens when leaders thrive, because thriving leaders find steadiness within themselves and do more than act with certainty. They remain open and seek inspiration from the world around them. It is this dual awareness that allows great leaders to move with both decisiveness and adaptability. They hold the ability to move with both conviction and flexibility, sensing when to hold firm and when to pivot, ensuring that the business evolves not through reaction, but through intent. It is about becoming the force that moves an organization and the world around it forward.

This is why embodied validation—the act of aligning mind and body—is often the missing link in leadership transformation. Projecting a future solely through intellect creates a disconnect. It is akin to stepping into a picture you have only observed, never inhabited. Without anchoring the body in the process, that future feels foreign—something external rather than something lived. This is where transformation either takes root or falls apart. If you remain mentally fixated on executing change without integrating it into your own being, you run the risk of finding yourself misaligned with the very movement you are trying to create.

13

LEADING WITH STRENGTH AND AGILITY

Every leader has a backbone—but not every leader has cultivated it. The spine serves as both a literal and a metaphorical foundation for how you move through the world. Physically, it provides structure, support, and mobility. Metaphorically, it represents the core of leadership: the ability to hold presence, stand firm while remaining flexible, and balance strength with adaptability. Conversely, a lack of strength in the spine responds to instability. Leadership is not just about direction; it is about how a leader stands, moves, and, through leadership, creates space for growth.

From a physiological standpoint, the spine does more than keep you upright. It houses the central nervous system, influencing how you process stress, respond to uncertainty, and hold presence in critical moments. The spine is a key conduit for embodied learning, transmitting signals that regulate movement, perception, and response. A mobile spine provides a foundation from which actions emerge with confidence and fluidity. Just as leaders under pressure often default to rigid control, mistaking tension for strength, a locked spine is an inflexible one. True leadership requires a spine that is strong yet fluid—able to stand firm in conviction but pivot when new realities emerge. The proprioceptive system—your ability to sense your body in space—is deeply linked to spinal function. This is why postural alignment and movement patterns directly affect cognitive clarity and emotional regulation. Research suggests that upright posture and spinal alignment influence neurological function, affecting decision-making and stress resilience. Studies in cognitive neuroscience have shown that slumped posture correlates with decreased confidence and increased stress, while an upright posture enhances cognitive processing and emotional stability.[1] Leaders who engage in embodied practices—exercise that creates movement and posture awareness—train not just their body but their capacity to process complex information and navigate pressure effectively. Much like how core strength enhances spinal support, embodied learning builds resilience in leadership by creating a felt sense of knowledge—one that is carried in muscle memory rather than just stored as intellectual theory. Centering yourself and physically aligning the spine through intentional focus and body awareness can stimulate oxytocin release, enhancing self-connection, personal power, and emotional regulation. This fosters a sense of safety, grounding, and trust—enabling you to approach change from a position of strength rather than fear.

In leadership and in management, we often talk about having each other's backs, and where this can create a sense of comfort and an initial boost of strength, the reality is that if support comes from an external source, it also risks weakening your own spine over time. Just like a corset may hold you upright, if worn too long, it will weaken your ability to stand on your own. This is also why competition is good, why ecosystems must remain dynamic, and why challenge and change have such huge potential to make you stronger.

Having someone's back is not a binary point. We can and should gain strength from each other at all stages of leadership and life. However, nurturing your own strength to stand grounded ahead of when it is needed enables you to lead, support, and pivot without risking the loss of your own strength and value. Research shows that learning through the body—whether through movement, posture, or action—creates stronger neural connections and deeper retention than intellectual processing alone.[2] This is why embodied leadership is not just a concept but a practice. For instance, physically experiencing freedom within a framework builds an internal experience of balancing structure with flexibility. The phrase is often used in business, yet without a personal grasp of what constitutes framework and where freedom lies, it can lead to hesitation in stepping beyond boundaries or a misinterpretation that results in chaos rather than contribution and progress.

I had been aware of these facts for some time, yet I also remember when they were truly cemented in my understanding. I have always loved to dance, and it has served me well throughout my life. At a point in my life when things were not unfolding as I had planned, I felt an urge to turn back to the reward of those moments. I hired a private instructor, determined to recapture the lightness I seemed to have misplaced. It felt great, it physically recharged me, and I returned to my day-to-day challenges with renewed energy. I learned that when my body felt safe, I gained strength to carry more in life. I loved these moments.

But a few years later, I felt the difference when this was flipped to something that enabled me to thrive. I started training with a new teacher. A teacher who, when he trained, embodied both the strength and the quiet depth I had come to recognize in truly exceptional leaders. He had the rare ability to balance structure and determination—driving performance to a global championship level—while remaining so attuned and grounded that he could hear every breath within the music, and the ability to bring it together to create something magnetic. At first, I was expecting the recharge, as I had before, to come from being effortlessly carried around the floor. However, this turned out not to be the case. Instead of just filling a deficit of feeling light, a familiar pattern in the fast-paced corporate life, I was challenged to redefine my strength. To stand on my own two feet. To discover what enabled me to stand stronger and ground myself. Refusing to default into old patterns enabled me to rewire my sense of structure and become fully complete within myself without dependency on external reinforcement.

This shift enabled me to hold an emotional awareness and actively decide how to deploy it, whether to wait in anticipation, walk with conviction, or simply project energy forward creating the space for others to step in. It was no longer about clinging onto glimpses of lightness or waiting to be led but about skillfully mastering oppositions. Not just recognizing the difference between charging and controlling a pause, between structure and flow, active and still, pushing forward and holding, standing firm and yielding, commanding space and giving it, but also having all these seeming opposites comfortably coexist at all times.

Instead of a moment of being carried, I cemented my ability to lead from within. Not just in dance but in life. This enabled me, in time, to no longer just follow the teachers' lead—I was shaping his growth, too, helping him grow true excellence beyond structure and process, by merging commitment with openness and strength with the ability to create space for others without losing ourselves. As leaders, we not only grow ourselves; we also help others grow.

My visioning, as ever, was sharp—my posture aligned, my gaze expansive, attuned to movement yet anchored in direction. My breath expanded—creating space for growth, setting a rhythm for others to connect into, and driving my energy forward. My arms and limbs moved decisively, not by force, but as an extension of a deeper inner alignment. And at the center of it all, my spine carried me forward unwavering yet adaptable, open to leading or being led, without ever losing power. This wasn't just movement; it was an ability to strategically deploy myself to create the greatest impact. And it is not about dancing, it is leadership in motion.

LEADING WITH PRESENCE AND INTENT

Just as in movement, leadership is not about holding a fixed position; it is the dynamic interplay that encourages interactions. The awareness of this strength is valuable within a business. Effective leaders actively shift between leading from the front when articulating ambition with clarity, to leading from behind when creating space for teams and partners to contribute and expand the potential, to leading from the side when fostering shared ownership with peers. Each of these has its place in leadership, but when deployed in the wrong context, they can be detrimental. Most leaders have trained extensively in leading from the front.

Leading from the front demands conviction. Leading from behind requires trust. Leading from the side fosters shared ownership. The key is knowing when to shift between them. Most leaders will have a preference, and those who lead from their spine have built agility that enables this to become a strength. However, leading from behind requires a different mastery, one that goes beyond delegation and into sensing, shaping, and subtly guiding outcomes without feeling threatened on our center.

> **Leading from the front demands conviction. Leading from behind requires trust. Leading from the side fosters shared ownership. The key is knowing when to shift between them.**

Leading from behind does not mean stepping away. It is not passive; it is a deliberate balance of empowerment and accountability. Those who lead from behind remain alert—actively sensing shifts, offering course corrections when needed, and making the tough decisions that keep the team aligned with the organization's ambition.[3] This form of leadership is not about detachment but about ensuring that others can step up without losing the guardrails that keep the business on course.

Interestingly, true control over leading from behind does not limit a leader—it expands their range. A leader who has mastered the ability to sense, stabilize, and generate momentum from behind is often the most capable of leading from any position. When the spine is actively engaged—not just metaphorically but physically, through the actual sensation of its presence along your back—it creates the confidence and stability to move seamlessly between the different forms of leadership. Those who truly understand how to lead from behind often find themselves more adept at leading from the front and the side as well, because they have learned to control movement of people not through dominance, but through precision, presence, and intent.

Have you ever tried to think about how you stand when leading? Are you locked? Do you physically hold yourself back, despite words calling for people to move? Or do you lean in with the head from the weight of the knowledge you hold? Or maybe do you let arms and gestures take center stage, frantically creating activity in the space around you?

I have sometimes asked leadership teams to draw themselves as a stickman—cut into three parts: the head, the torso, and the legs—without giving further context.[4] I then ask them to share whether they believe they lead change headfirst, followed by the rest, or legs first, or how. Interestingly, most people think that the correct answer is to say you lead with your head, wisely thinking through what to do and then moving. Others proudly share that they move with pace and try things; therefore, they choose legs first followed by head. A few, often the HR person in the room, will say they lead with their heart and what feels right and therefore draw the torso ahead of the other parts. Unfortunately, very rarely do leaders acknowledge the limitations of creating followership from the spine and how this in fact makes the head sharper and the legs faster.

When a leader is truly grounded from within, they do not fear openness because they know they will not be knocked down by it. They can listen without losing focus, adjust without losing intent, channel feelings to where they add value, and create an environment in which others can move with them and remain fully present without compromising their direction.

HOW CONTEXT SHAPES PERCEPTION

Just as the spine needs training to remain physically agile, even the strongest leadership spine requires continuous appropriate resistance to stay adaptable rather than becoming rigid. Unfortunately, occasionally we see leaders who over time build such an unquestioned center of gravity that those around them begin to anchor their bias around the leader's fixed position. In the most serious of cases, this concentrated authority breeds loyalty by fear, shifting the focus from sensing opportunities to seeking approval.

This is why seeking out new perspectives is not just a business prerequisite to capture business and technology shifts but a fundamental requirement for sustained, embodied leadership. Growth in businesses requires a stretch, and if leaders themselves do not train their brains to expand, they should not expect the collective capabilities to reach further either. Generative conversations, diverse teams, ecosystems, and technology all can grow your perspective, but just as you need to understand the intent, value, and benefit to those engaging with you and your business gain, it is even more essential to discern the intent of those helping you shape your leadership.

It's essential to seek out perspectives that stretch your thinking without pulling it off its course and to know the difference between insight that sharpens your leadership and noise that feeds distraction or builds doubt.

I have personally experienced how context shapes perception. As a kid in school, I experienced how other kids could judge me as the quiet student, leading to me being easily overlooked, to another school, where I—the same person in a different setting—was suddenly recognized as determined and very capable. This embodied experience channeled right has proved incredibly valuable since and shown how critical understanding and building perspective is. Many years later, as part of my corporate career, I transitioned into a new environment where the unspoken social hierarchies were already in place. The in-crowd had formed long before I arrived, and I quickly realized I wasn't part of it. At first, I felt the sting of exclusion—the quiet conversations I was not invited into, the inside jokes I didn't understand, and the subtle but clear sense that I was on the outside looking in. It wasn't easy, but as I moved past my initial emotional response, I felt the huge value in being outside the immediate flow. From this position, I could see the bigger picture, how influence moved, and which dynamics mattered with such clarity. Some might call it corporate astuteness or organizational savvy, but as a leader in the midst of the action, it's difficult to keep that perspective clear and unclouded. This also speaks to the power of a correctly framed perspective. This situation was not something to feel victimized by; instead, it was about understanding the opportunities and actively deploying these for further success.

Perspective is a choice. This is an important leadership lesson. It is a choice you can fuel, such as I did, having chosen to build expertise by seeing the world from many different vantage points, industries, and ownership structures; work in multiple continents; study at Copenhagen Business School, Stanford, INSEAD, IMD, and MIT; make friends from all layers of life; and continue to remain curious to grow. But it can also be fueled by focusing attention to step onto the balcony. To detach from the immediate noise, actively avoiding group think, and allowing space to sense steps and patterns before they fully emerge. Not only does this allow us as leaders to look at skill gaps, examine new competency connections, sense the pace of change, and so on, but it will also enable emotional disconnection from the crowds shaping the narrative as it is experienced on the crowded floor.

Leadership is always a balance of introspection and external awareness. But the right answers—for you and your business—are never found in external understanding alone, just as growth doesn't come from looking inward in isolation. The key lies in grounded, embodied leadership that strengthens your perspective and sharpens your ability to navigate forward with clarity. I've found that leadership today often means moving from meeting to meeting with people seeking to shape my opinions. Holding a balcony view requires personal discipline, curated learning, and ideally a select group of trusted voices. It is not just about seeking advice—hence surrounding myself with leaders who hold experience but lack self-awareness, which can create an even stronger risk than not seeking advice at all—but about having advisors who bring perspective *without agenda*, whether they are mentors, advisors, wingmen, or the quiet "CEO whisperers." People who observe from the edges ensure that while a leader stands firm, they do not become fixed. Most importantly, they give advice without judgment. These hold the role, much like my dance teacher did, of encouraging strength from within; of stretching; of reaching and showing persistence; of calling it when they see it, not just when asked; and of being ready to catch you if you fall. Even more, they feel true pride as you grow and stand stronger. Because it is not about them; it is about *us*.

EMBODY A WILLINGNESS TO EVOLVE

Leadership, at its core, is a constant negotiation between trust and change. Trust—in yourself, in others, and in the process of transformation—is essential. Without it, change can feel destabilizing rather than expansive. But trust must be balanced with perspective. It is not just about relying on those who shout the loudest for insight. It is about ensuring that trust does not become an echo chamber that limits adaptability.

Many leaders resist change not because they fear the unknown but because they overidentify with who they have been. More than a decade ago, data was brought forward to show a striking paradox: When asked, few people believe they are the same person they were ten years ago. And yet, when asked how much they expect to change in the next decade, most predict little to no transformation. This disconnect between our past evolution and our future expectations can be a silent inhibitor of growth. When we as leaders assume we have already become our "final version," we unintentionally limit our own adaptability.[5] But change does not need to be grand or sweeping to be transformative.

It is often small shifts—moments of stepping into something unfamiliar—that unlock new ways of thinking and moving forward. I witnessed this firsthand when running a global

> The challenge is not just balancing the demands of the present with the vision for the future but also recognizing where past patterns may be limiting what is possible next.

marketing function. During a large conference, I chose to bring one of my dance instructors in to do a brief session to kick off the second day, using movement as a way to anchor learning and to shift energy. Among the attendees was the global head of sales—a highly respected, traditional leader who excelled in his field but was at the time not known for experimenting with new approaches. I made a conscious decision not to look at him during the session, knowing this experience was likely uncomfortable for him. Afterward, however, he approached me and said it had been one of the most thought-provoking experiences he had ever had—one that made him reflect more deeply than any formal training course. What struck me was not just his willingness to participate but what happened after. That single moment of stepping beyond his comfort zone seemed to create a new openness, a shift in how he engaged with learning and change. Over time, I saw a new ability to challenge his own assumptions and embrace ideas beyond his usual frame of reference. This reinforced something I have seen throughout my career: Change is not something that happens to us—we shape it, but only if we are willing to engage with it. Every leader carries their own history, shaped by past decisions, experiences, and trade-offs. The challenge is not just balancing the demands of the present with the vision for the future but also recognizing where past patterns may be limiting what is possible next. And just as a strong spine enables movement rather than restricting it, true leadership stability comes not from rigidity but from dynamic strength, remaining grounded while allowing movement to flow. If you can integrate physical awareness into your learning and decision-making, you will be better able to maintain clarity during busyness, much like how a strong spine allows for both stability and mobility under physical strain. Whether in a high-pressure boardroom discussion or a moment of strategic reflection, if you embody your learning, you will move with more precision and confidence.

Because the world is moving at such pace, great leaders know that stability, in fact, stems from movement, from actively shaping the rhythm of transformation that positions us with and ahead of the market. They cultivate a cadence of change—one that balances identity with evolution and clarity with the openness to refine their perspectives. Transformation does not happen in a single moment—it is not an announcement, a decision, or an isolated success. It is an ongoing movement, a discipline of continuous alignment. Those who lead from their spine—who embody both presence and adaptability—don't just navigate change; they set the rhythm for it.

14

CHOOSING TO LEAD

Leadership, like life, comes with no clear recipe. You can gather inspiration, gain support, and surround yourself with a great team, but in fact one of the greatest edges lies in owning your own approach. Great wisdom lies in learning, yet leadership at its core is not imitation but more integration. When you move from externally seeking direction to becoming your own reference point is when true leadership happens.

Personally, I spent a large part of my life without clear role models—not because I lacked talented people around me but because none of their paths felt right to follow. It was never a matter of looking up and thinking, *I wish I could be like you.* There was always too big a trade-off, choices that, while right for them, did not align with what I needed to be. It became clear to me that true leadership wasn't about fitting into an existing mold; it was about building the conviction to stand fully in my own. Even businesses that achieve market dominance or profitability by following others do not simply replicate—they succeed by understanding what sets them apart. Whether refining an approach, challenging select assumptions, or executing with sharper precision, their strength lies in acute awareness of their own strengths. Leadership is no different. It is not about choosing between existing paths but about defining your own with clarity and intent.

> If you walk the same path as others, you will end up only where others have been—and it will feel like them, not like you.

This taught me to become my own role model, making choices that paved the way for the future as best as possible. Choosing to become your own role model is not about striving for an idealized version of yourself, but about cultivating a deep understanding of your values, strengths, and aspirations, and navigating forward with this—as is the case for the business you lead. Even more, this acceptance has made me a stronger strategic business leader, one who has proudly and repeatedly delivered successes ahead of the market. Not becoming comfortable by having someone's shoes to walk in means constantly being curious and open to seeing what opportunities are out there, strategically making the step that you see the highest potential in. Many leaders will hopefully recognize this, at least in parts of their lives, and this is exactly the same as winning with venturing. If you walk the same path as others, you will end up only where others have been—and it will feel like them, not like you.

SHAPING YOUR NARRATIVE

When faced with seemingly insurmountable change, both in life and in business, I choose to approach it as if it were a strategic business task at hand. I always start reconnecting with my ambition and then step back and look at all the elements in front of me, assessing which data points deserve a role in my future and treating each one as part of a larger puzzle. Always anchored in the truth, both the truth I see and one that others will comfortably validate, but this does not mean all elements deserve equal weight. Then, I start to shape a narrative that allows me to see a clear path forward. It is not about jumping on what first comes to mind, but as in any business strategy shaping hypothesis, shaped by knowing your direction, acknowledging where you are now, and then finding proof points and relevant stepstones toward the ambition. Once I have started to see a pattern emerge, I try saying it out loud—I sit with it, reflect on it, and ask myself if it holds up. Does it feel authentic as well as feasible, desirable, and viable? Does it make sense in the context of where I am now and where I want to go? I may put it on a slide, but it must always be strong enough for me to be able to remember by heart at any hour of the day, or I have not found the right narrative yet.

I share it in conversation with trusted partners or colleagues or, if it is a personal narrative, with friends. At first, not to get their reactions but to validate how it sits with me. If I allow others to define my story or prioritize their version of events, it will be much harder for me to embody it. After starting with those close to me, I test my story next with people I know will oppose and, ideally, some people who do not know me or my business at all. I listen for reactions and questions, considering not just what they actually say but what made them say this. If they question feasibility, it is maybe a lack of articulation of what has built my skills and conviction, or it could be a representation of their own fears projected onto me. If the challenge is about viability, I have likely not adequately linked the external currents into my narrative, and if they do not find it desirable, it is normally very easy to sense whether that means it is just not for them and there is ample place for me and my business, or I have not been ambitious enough. All will give me great feedback to help refine and strengthen, and when you have a good narrative, you immediately recognize how people connect it to their own, build on it, and extend it much as a business ecosystem growing. By owning and shaping your own narrative, you own your leadership, whether in business or in life. In this way, any mountain ahead of me—no matter how daunting—becomes manageable. I own the direction, and I move with conviction.

We also shape narratives while we live them, just as businesses venture. But to make sure this does not send me astray, I sense-check my narrative on a regular basis—when anything major happens or at least once a year.

I encourage others to do the same, both for themselves and for their business. Hopefully, you will find that your business becomes a proof point on your personal narrative, and your personal becomes a proof point on your business narrative. If not, you need to question whether you are deploying yourself right. When narratives compete and truths blur, know that your story is always yours to shape, provided you stay honest and open to others' validation. Owning your journey—acknowledging facts, learning from setbacks, adjusting pace, and separating emotion from decisions—builds both authenticity and momentum. This clarity empowers you to navigate complexity, seize opportunities, and embrace uncertainty as a catalyst for growth. This approach transforms uncertainty into opportunity and helps navigate change with resilience.

Change is inevitable—but by taking control of your story, you shape it, ride with it, and define it on your own terms. I personally welcome being moved, but I decide whether to accept the invitation or not. I read the movement around me, but when I step forward, I step with conviction and clarity for others. Grounded leaders actively choose to guide with steadiness and conviction, creating space for others to step in. Authentic leadership enables others to thrive.

FROM CONCEPT TO REALITY

A strong spine and a well-crafted narrative remain unnoticed unless actively brought to life. Many great business ideas never reach their intended impact, not because they lack merit but because they are not effectively translated into action. Throughout this book, we have explored the importance of seeing further to define a vision, expanding thinking to sustain momentum, actively steering toward success, and leading with intent. The scope of this may appear daunting, yet just as those who are busy often manage to achieve more, the way energy is mobilized determines whether ambitions transition from concept to reality.

Driven by intellectual curiosity and an openness to explore perspectives beyond the traditional business world, I had sought out a session with a quantum physics professor. The topic? Energy, not just in the scientific sense but as something that shapes how we move through the world, lead, and create momentum. I didn't go in expecting direct answers for leadership, but as I listened, I realized his perspective helped validate the patterns I had seen in practice.

He explained that we are all made of energy and our personal frequencies are influenced by thoughts, emotions, and actions. Positive emotions such as joy, gratitude, and momentum emit higher frequency energy waves. If you looked at them on a graph, they would show up as nice, big, soft waves, much like the way a child would draw the ocean. These waves can invite others to join your rhythm, and together, the waves align and move at greater height and strength. Exactly what you want for any transformation.

Negative emotions, such as fear and anger, emit lower vibrational and frequency energy waves and can puncture the larger, softer waves and break the rhythm. However, they cannot create momentum and followership. A closed mind—a punctuating wavelength—is also one that is disproportionately filled with its own strength and voice and therefore does not give space for being open. Or what about the physiological reactions? Anger often involves a shift in heart rate, more intense breathing, tense shoulders, and hormone release—all of which are likely to be more energy-draining for you. In getting angry, you are letting the moment drain you instead of mobilizing attention toward the positive opportunity.

Positive waves are punctured all the time in business—even by well-intended and timely comments such as "Today's priority agenda is . . ." or "Investors are struggling to understand . . . ." As a leader, how often do you think about how to restart the positive energy waves to get the motivation and momentum you inadvertently just killed?

Energy is contagious—both negative and positive energy. And it's not just about motion but about resonance. And just as both you and companies strategically deploy financial resources, so your energy must also be deployed strategically. The most effective leaders don't just focus on where they invest their energy, but also on where they deliberately step back and allow others to take ownership and drive momentum. Leadership is not about being at the center of every movement, but about ensuring energy flows in the right places. Research on emotional transference has demonstrated that emotions spread within groups, influencing productivity, decision-making, and engagement.[1] High-frequency emotions such as enthusiasm and optimism have been linked to increased collaboration and innovation in organizations.[2] Conversely, negative emotional contagion can dampen engagement and create decision paralysis.

I once led a very diverse team—consisting of, among others, strategists, creatives, developers, and lead generators—in our open plan office. Our immediate neighbors were a customer service recovery team, largely consisting of lawyers. Not long after we moved into our spot, they asked us to lower our voices, because we laughed too much. Respectfully, I naturally enquired whether it limited their focus, or whether customers could hear it through the phone while discussing distressing matters, but there was none of this. Instead, they just found our laughing odd. While I was reminded that energy is also contextual and depends on cultural expectations and so on, I was pleased when the team started coming over to talk. The inviting tone of our conversations, odd as it was to them, was also welcoming and eventually led to some great business challenges being solved together.

Instead of concentrating momentum in singular moments, think about where to place the most infectious energy across the organization—ensuring that transformation is not an occasional spark, but an ongoing current that sustains long-term progress.

WINNING BY DESIGN

The tangible rewards of business transformation are undeniable. Studies show that companies that embrace transformation effectively are 2.5 times more likely to outperform their peers in profitability and long-term growth.[3] And while many struggle with transformation, those who succeed—outperforming their peers in profitability and long-term growth—are the ones who combine a strong strategic ambition with the right leadership, execution, and culture.[4] Sustainable change doesn't happen by accident, it happens by design. Leadership design.

It is not simply about responding to change when the moment demands it, but about choosing transformation as an ongoing discipline. The best leaders don't wait for certainty, they step forward with conviction, embracing the unknown as an integral part of progress. True leadership requires the courage to act before the full picture is clear, to shape direction rather than wait for permission. It is about standing firm in what is essential while remaining open to what must evolve—a principle that is reflected in the very way we carry ourselves, hold our presence, and how we move.

The smallest choices often set the greatest transformations in motion. I recall a dinner last year, surrounded by some of the world's most remarkable minds—board chairs, CEOs, founders of world-defining companies, artists, and an opera singer. At one point, the singer stood up and demonstrated something seemingly simple, yet profound. He held a wine glass by its stem and then gently tapped it with a fork. The glass rang out with a clear, resonant tone. Then, he grasped it by its bowl and tapped again—the sound was stifled, short, and lifeless.

With this small gesture, he made a powerful point: When we grip too tightly—whether to an idea, a position, or control itself—we limit its potential. Yet a grip that is too loose leads to instability. Leadership is no different. The way leaders hold their vision, their people, and their decisions determines whether momentum is created or cut short.

Leadership is not a destination—it is a continuous pursuit. The legacy of a leader is not written in a single moment, but in the rhythm of choices made over time. The question is never whether change will come—the question is, will it move through you or *because* of you?

Part IV Reflections to Motivate Action:
Are You Embodying as You Lead in Motion?

Leadership in motion is meeting change with open eyes, expansive breath, and steady hands—moving with clarity, so others feel ready to step forward with you.

- *Shedding outdated narratives:* Which narratives—about yourself, your team, or your industry—are still shaped by outdated thinking, and how intentionally are you choosing to reinforce a new reality instead?

- *Training to thrive, not just survive:* What practices are you putting in place to sustain strength, energy, and awareness—so that you, and your team, stay capable of leading through pressure without losing clarity or momentum?

- *Grounded in motion:* When leading through change, are you grounded enough to balance presence, adaptability, and sensing—so your teams can stay attuned, responsive, and committed to forward momentum?

Conclusion

THE ANATOMY OF GROWTH

B usiness success is not determined by activity but by the ability to channel effort into meaningful outcomes. At the core of this ability lies leadership—how decisions are made, how direction is set, and how a well-calibrated ambition translates into real impact.

The stories I have shared—of transformation, leadership, and the forces that enable or hinder progress—are not just lessons in business but invitations to step into a space of clarity and conviction. Leadership is about recognizing patterns, creating space for growth, mobilizing action, and standing firm in what truly matters. It is not about following predetermined paths but rather about shaping them. True leadership means refusing to settle, resisting the pull of external definitions of success, and forging a course that aligns with both personal integrity and business impact. It is a privileged space—not one granted by title but earned through action.

As leaders, we know that growth—whether in leadership or business—is not a set formula to follow but a responsibility to embrace. That is why I am grateful that so many leaders have shaped the stories in this book. And fortunately, many more companies out there continue to prove this thinking. Progress is not about celebrating one but about expanding with curiosity and deploying with conviction.

In business today, still too often, in the search for quick fixes, I have seen leaders push tighter, grasping for simple tools rather than unfolding the full potential of themselves and their business. Instead of just calling for more leads, could those pursuing top-line growth step back and ask: Are we visioning far enough to set the right trajectory? Are we being expansive enough to ride the momentum of market growth? And when the pressure is on to protect margins, do we steer decisively, ensuring energy is focused where it matters most? Or do we take the time to explore whether expanding could, in fact, reveal smarter paths, whether from within or through the ecosystem?

Fortunately, the stories are many more; there are global references such as those who inspired us about visioning: Apple, which redefined our take on personal computers and devices; Amazon, which showed the world the concept of a platform; Spotify, which changed the music industry; and MercadoLibre, which saw a gap in the financial infrastructure and grew from retailer to fintech. These are all great examples of venturing. When you envision, you can capture patterns earlier, see further, anticipate shifts, and define opportunities ahead of the market. Leaders who master this don't just react to change—they shape it.

We have seen excellence in expansive thinking from many companies beyond what I have already referred to in the book, such as retail leaders like Inditex (brand owner of Zara, Pull&Bear, and others), which has mastered fast, localized fashion and innovative production by staying attuned to local contributions. From Siemens, which has transformed from an industrial manufacturer into a leader in automation and smart infrastructure, and Alibaba, which we have all followed as it continues to scale through its ecosystem, leveraging partnerships and platform thinking. All demonstrate that true expansion is built on empowerment, platform thinking, strategic agility, and deep awareness strengths—growing in ways that make them stronger and more future-proof, not just larger.

And for those of you who connected with the steering part of this book, where I show firsthand how clarity and proactive alignment between execution and strategy make all the difference, there are companies that are wisely and decisively attuning actions to ambition, such as Schneider Electric, which strengthened cross-functional collaboration, ingested critical skills, and built a compelling internal and external change story. Or P&G, which uses data-driven decision-making not just for execution models and product portfolios but also for talent allocation, maximizing both efficiency and impact. Steering ensures that vision and expansion don't meander but instead become deeply embedded in business operations and results.

I also explore embodiment—where leadership, culture, and execution become generative, and natural followership emerges. Role-model businesses demonstrate this effortlessly: Disney, delivering storytelling across eras and formats without wavering in its core identity; Ferrari, steadfast in its commitment to performance and exclusivity; and NASA, which, even when shifting from government-led missions to collaborative partnerships with private industry and spinning off businesses, has remained anchored in exploration and pushing human potential. I've found that embodied businesses and leaders step into change with conviction and calm. We are attuned to soft signals of change, welcome invitations to move, and choose each step with confidence, grounded in our core.

The strongest businesses—and leaders—don't just excel in one of these areas; they integrate them all. Think about how companies such as LEGO, Toyota, and Netflix demonstrate leadership by combining visioning, expansion, steering, and strong embodiment. While they, too, waver at times, their strength lies in knowing that leadership is not about any single decision but about continuously reinforcing multiple leadership muscles—ensuring they don't just survive change but actively drive it. All three of these companies significantly outperform their peers on profitability.

I hope the stories and perspectives shared in this book have reinforced that the strongest businesses—and the strongest leaders—do not rely on isolated elements of their leadership anatomy. Sustainable, profitable growth is not about excelling at a single lever but about integrating them all with intent. By now, this should feel less like theory and more like an invitation—an active choice to steer toward a stronger future. Leadership deepens with curiosity, sharpens with self-awareness, and strengthens through practice. For some of you, this will mean investing in your identity and deploying it with greater precision. For others, it will be about positioning your business for exponential growth, leveraging technology not just as an enabler but as a strategic force.

This is all possible. Some stories in this book may come from global corporations, but the principles behind them apply anywhere. Whether it is reading market and ecosystem shifts, investing in what sets you apart, or surrounding yourself with the right people to excel, these aren't privileges reserved for a select few. These are choices, habits, and ways of thinking that can be lived in any context. No matter where you are today, the opportunity to shape what comes next is within reach. And at the heart of every great business are the leaders who make that choice.

Leadership deepens with curiosity, sharpens with self-awareness, and strengthens through practice.

Just as businesses have their natural strengths and journey into this, so do we. Strength in one area is never enough—lasting success, transformation, and impact demand all four. The best leaders ensure their business masters visioning, expanding, steering, and embodying, and I've found that true leadership fulfillment comes from engaging meaningfully with all. While teams, when adequately supported and empowered, can extend a leader's capabilities in the first three, embodiment can never be outsourced. It is the foundation that anchors all the rest. As leaders, we don't just deliver and transform, we inspire others who want to follow. We live it.

Winning in business and in life begins with you.

Appendix

LEADERSHIP ANATOMY MIRROR

S tories stay with us, not just in what we hear but in what we feel and apply. I hope the experiences shared and perspectives raised have resonated—and that you've already started drawing connections to your own context.

Moving from thinking to action requires both understanding and focus. To support this shift, versions of the questions shared at the end of each part are captured here in Table A.1, which is designed to help you reflect on your current *leadership anatomy in motion* and identify what you will strengthen to win in the future. And are you feeling the value of confidence to lead through both technology and people, in business and in life?

It's a dual reflection:

- The strength of your personal leadership

- The ability and readiness of your business

Each axis represents a critical dimension of transformation. Score each one from 1 to 5, both as an individual leader and from your business's perspective:

1. Not part of your mind space

2. Novice but learning

3. On par with peers

4. Selectively leading

5. Defining change/role model

Once you've completed your scoring—both for yourself and for your business—plot your results on the chart in Figure A.1. Step back and look at the shape of your results. This isn't just about the scores; it's about what they reveal. Figure A.2 shows an example of a completed chart.

Now, take a moment to reflect on what the results reveal. Use the following reflections to help you explore what the results tell you and where you can leverage your leadership anatomy more effectively.

- *Understanding natural strengths:* Where are your greatest strengths—in visioning, expanding, steering, and embodying? Look at this both as an individual and across your business. The areas not achieving leading levels—have they been underdeveloped, under-resourced, or simply overlooked? Are your strengths typical of your peers, industry, or sector? Are you ready to share your leadership anatomy in motion with your teams and partners?

- *Understanding current position versus desire:* Is this the footprint you wish to leave behind? Is this who you wish to be—as a person, a leader, and for your business? If not, what would you like it to be? And how will you be enabling the shifts?

TABLE A.1: LEADERSHIP REFLECTION QUESTIONS

		BUSINESS	SCORE (1–5)	INDIVIDUAL	SCORE (1–5)
VISIONING	1. Ambition as the loudest voice for action	How does your compelling and inspiring big ambition serve as a focal point for your team, motivating them to see beyond their daily tasks and look to a higher potential?		How does your compelling and inspiring big ambition serve as a focal point for you, motivating you to see beyond the daily pressures and look to a higher potential?	
	2. Clarity on core capability	Are you crystal clear on, if your company was an AI, which capability it would guide? Or looking at it differently, is everyone aware of which part of your proposition is so essential that it must be nurtured and can be deployed in a future ecosystem?		What personal capabilities are so core to your value that they must be continuously nurtured and build your identity beyond your current role?	
	3. Anticipating and acting on emerging signals	Are you aware of which wakes you will ride and how often your strategic choices lift and shape the market—rather than try to fit in after someone has defined the rules?		Are you great at seeing, capturing, and being curious about infant signals before others—and consciously deciding whether to bring them into your success?	
EXPANDING	4. Recognized ecosystem value	Which players (partners, competitors, customers, etc.) in your ecosystem hold valuable learning data that could accelerate your path toward your ambition? And what would they gain from partnering with you?		Have you created an ecosystem for yourself (professionally, societally, and personally) that lifts and challenges your thinking—and are you great at growing others in return?	
	5. Rewarding catalytic conversations	How are you recognizing and rewarding those who build on existing knowledge—rather than starting from scratch?		Have you created space for thought-generating conversations today? And are you consistently inviting more of these?	
	6. Expanding with intention and courage	To what extent does your organization challenge its own assumptions and foster a culture where curiosity and openness drive decision-making?		To what extent do you intentionally keep your thinking open—challenging assumptions and inviting fresh input before pressure demands it—so your decisions stay relevant and your momentum is guided by awareness, not familiarity?	

continued

		BUSINESS	SCORE (1-5)	INDIVIDUAL	SCORE (1-5)
STEERING	7. Deliberate support for change allies	Who will be the fast followers of your change agents, and are you actively supporting them?		Are you yourself a lone mover, a fast follower, or waiting for the crowd? And is this what you wish to be?	
	8. Talent aligned to future needs	Is your business staffed for the past or the future? And how are you actively and consistently signaling your future expectations through placing and supporting people?		Do your current skills and focus reflect where you want to lead—and how actively are you inviting people to complement you where you are still growing?	
	9. Metrics that matter	Are your KPIs creating confinement or collaboration? Are the metrics encouraging learning and cross-functional progress—or limiting them?		What actions have you taken this week to uncover insights across silos and hierarchies? And have then shifted metrics accordingly?	
EMBODYING	10. Shedding outdated narratives	Are narratives—about your business, your teams, or your industry—still rooted in outdated thinking? Have you identified who created these? And is your business reinforcing or showing a different reality?		Are you aware of which narratives about yourself are still rooted in outdated thinking? Have you identified the emotions driving this? Do they still deserve this impact?	
	11. Training to thrive, not just survive	Is your organization training to thrive—or just helping people survive the daily pressures?		Are you training to thrive or just to survive—and how consistently have you brought this to your presence and leadership today?	
	12. Grounded in motion	To what extent does your organization move from a centered place—grounded in intent, alert to change, with everyone aligned and personally invested in the outcome?		Do you hold steady in motion—present, alert, sensing, and ready to act—while being clear on what is truly in it for you? Or do you freeze or fall when pushed?	

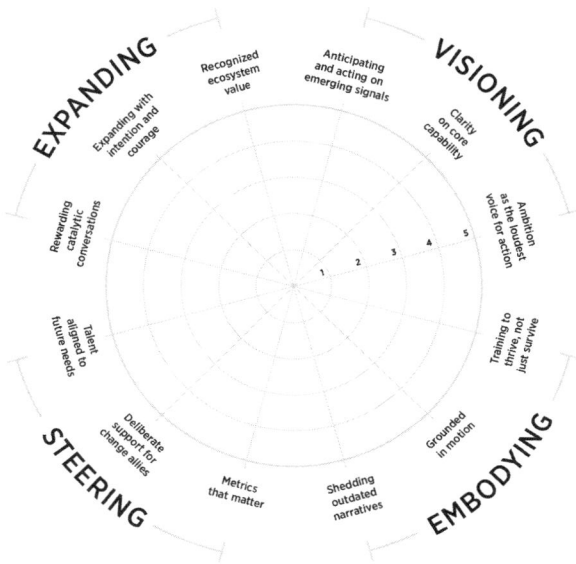

Figure A.1: Leadership anatomy self-assessment chart

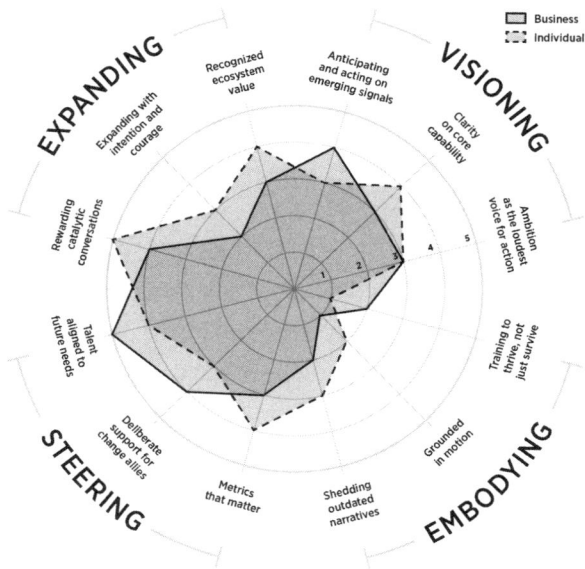

Figure A.2: Example of a completed self-assessment chart

- *Understanding business and individual alignment:* How do your scores compare between yourself and your business? If the business consistently leads, consider whether leadership needs to create more space—through trust, empowerment, or personal risk-taking. If leadership leads but the business lags, ask honestly: *What am I enabling?* Are your insights being translated into systems, decisions, and action? And have you intentionally staffed or partnered in areas where your strengths need reinforcement, while ensuring this doesn't remove your responsibility to continue growing in those areas?

If you're consistently scoring 4s and 5s, congratulations—you're not just keeping pace; you're shaping the future and actively navigating in motion. You may be a fit for a future book or knowledge-sharing initiative featuring transformative leaders in action. I would love to hear from you.

If your scores are more mixed, this is not a weakness—it is a signal. These are not gaps to be judged, but gifts to be addressed. Each one holds insight into an opportunity—to strengthen your position and unlock greater impact by deploying your existing strengths more effectively.

My advisory work exists to help leaders raise their awareness and strengthen their capacity to lead through both people and technology—anchored in presence, shaped by insight, and geared toward action that matters. Whether navigating complexity, sharpening priorities, or building stronger collaboration across silos, the aim is to evolve leadership from static control to embodied motion. If you're ready to lead with curiosity, empathy, clarity, and conviction, you're welcome to book a session and evolve your leadership anatomy in motion.

For more illustrations, resources, and opportunities to connect, visit www.leadershipanatomyinmotion.com or www.louisaloran.com.

NOTES

INTRODUCTION

1. Donald Sull, Charles Sull, and James Yoder, "No One Knows Your Strategy—Not Even Your Top Leaders," *MIT Sloan Management Review*, February 12, 2018, https://sloanreview.mit.edu/article/no-one-knows-your-strategy-not-even-your-top-leaders/.

2. Roger Martin, "The Signs of a Good CEO," *Medium*, October 7, 2024, https://rogermartin.medium.com/the-signs-of-a-good-ceo-160a73656cf9.

CHAPTER 1

1. Data from internal company records, 2023.

2. Adam Burden, Edwin Van der Ouderaa, Ramnath Venkataraman, Tomas Nyström, and Prashant P. Shukla, "Technical Debt Might Be Hindering Your Digital Transformation," *MIT Sloan Management Review*, June 19, 2018, https://sloanreview.mit.edu/article/technical-debt-might-be-hindering-your-digital-transformation.

CHAPTER 2

1. McKinsey & Company, "Unlocking Success in Digital Transformations," October 29, 2018, https://www.mckinsey.com/capabilities/people-and-organizational-performance/our-insights/unlocking-success-in-digital-transformations.

2.   Bain & Company, "88% of Business Transformations Fail to Achieve Their Original Ambitions; Those That Succeed Avoid Overloading Top Talent," April 15, 2024, https://www.bain.com/about/media-center/press-releases/2024/88-of -business-transformations-fail-to-achieve-their-original-ambitions-those-that -succeed-avoid-overloading-top-talent/.

3.   Patrick Forth, Tom Reichert, Romain de Laubier, and Saibal Chakraborty, "Flipping the Odds of Digital Transformation Success," Boston Consulting Group, October 29, 2020, https://www.bcg.com/publications/2020/ increasing-odds-of-success-in-digital-transformation.

4.   Ray Oldenburg, *The Great Good Place: Cafés, Coffee Shops, Bookstores, Bars, Hair Salons, and Other Hangouts at the Heart of a Community* (Da Capo, 1989).

5.   Renault Group, "Renaulution: A Four-Year Plan to Transform Our Group," accessed April 14, 2025, https://www.renaultgroup.com/en/group/our-strategy.

6.   "Renault Is Unlikely Role Model for European Autos," *Financial Times*, March 5, 2025, https://www.ft.com/content/dedff337-a275-442a-82e6 -e531de82468c.

CHAPTER 3

1.   Bloomberg Billionaires Index, "Today's Billionaires," accessed March 10, 2025, https://www.bloomberg.com/billionaires/.

2.   Edelman, "2024 Edelman Trust Barometer Reveals Innovation Has Become a New Risk Factor for Trust," January 14, 2024, https://www.edelman.com/ news-awards/2024-edelman-trust-barometer.

3.   PwC, "PwC's 2024 Trust Survey: 8 Key Findings," March 12, 2024, https://www.pwc.com/us/en/library/trust-in-business-survey.html.

4.   Brené Brown, *Dare to Lead: Brave Work, Tough Conversations, Whole Hearts* (Random House, 2018), 71.

5.   Albert Bandura, *Social Cognitive Theory: An Agentic Perspective on Human Nature*, ed. Daniel Cervone (Wiley, 2023).

CHAPTER 4

1.   John-Anthony Disotto, "You'll Soon Be Able to Use Gemini in Apple Intelligence as iOS 18.4 Beta Hints at Upcoming Integration," *TechRadar*, February 24, 2025, https://www.techradar.com/computing/artificial-intelligence/youll-soon-be-able-to -use-gemini-in-apple-intelligence-as-ios-18-4-beta-hints-at-upcoming-integration.

2.   Ashish Vaswani, Noam Shazeer, Niki Parmar, et al., "Attention Is All You Need," *Proceedings of the 31st International Conference on Neural Information Processing Systems* (2017): 5998–6008, https://proceedings.neurips.cc/paper_files/paper/2017/file/3f5ee243547dee91fbd053c1c4a845aa-Paper.pdf.

3.   Leroy Hood and Lee Rowen, "The Human Genome Project: Big Science Transforms Biology and Medicine," *Genome Medicine* 5, no. 9 (2013), https://pmc.ncbi.nlm.nih.gov/articles/PMC4066586/.

4.   Statista, "Market Capitalization of Toyota Worldwide from 2010 to 2023," accessed March 10, 2025, https://www.statista.com/statistics/279650/market-capitalization-of-toyota/.

5.   Melisa Cavcic, "Shell and ExxonMobil JV Cuts a Deal with Canadian Firm to Give Up Its North Sea Oil and Gas Business for $180 Million," *Offshore Energy*, July 19, 2024, https://www.offshore-energy.biz/shell-and-exxonmobil-jv-cuts-a-deal-with-canadian-firm-to-give-up-its-north-sea-oil-gas-business-for-180-million/.

CHAPTER 5

1.   Matthew D. Lieberman, *Social: Why Our Brains Are Wired to Connect* (Crown, 2013).

2.   John Sweller, "Cognitive Load During Problem Solving: Effects on Learning," *Cognitive Science* 12, no. 2 (1988): 257–285.

3.   Anita Williams Woolley, Christopher F. Chabris, Alex Pentland, Nada Hashmi, and Thomas W. Malone, "Evidence for a Collective Intelligence Factor in the Performance of Human Groups," *Science* 330, no. 6004 (2010): 686–688.

4.   Gallup, "The Benefits of Employee Engagement," *Gallup Workplace* (blog), January 7, 2023, https://www.gallup.com/workplace/236927/employee-engagement-drives-growth.aspx%20The%20Benefits%20of%20Employee%20Engagement.

CHAPTER 6

1.   Illustrations and resources can be found at www.leadershipanatomyinmotion.com.

2.   Julian Baggini, *How the World Thinks: A Global History of Philosophy* (Granta Books, 2018).

3.   Illustrations and resources can be found at www.leadershipanatomyinmotion.com.

CHAPTER 7

1. Daniel Kahneman and Amos Tversky, "Prospect Theory: An Analysis of Decision Under Risk," *Econometrica* 47, no. 2 (1979): 263–291.

2. Tara Swart, *The Source: The Secrets of the Universe, the Science of the Brain* (HarperOne, 2019).

3. John H. Zenger and Joseph Folkman, *The Extraordinary Leader: Turning Good Managers into Great Leaders* (McGraw-Hill, 2009).

CHAPTER 8

1. Alfonso Pulido, Dorian Stone, and John Strevel, "The Three Cs of Customer Satisfaction: Consistency, Consistency, Consistency," McKinsey & Company, March 1, 2014, https://www.mckinsey.com/industries/retail/our-insights/the-three-cs-of-customer-satisfaction-consistency-consistency-consistency#/.

2. Dan Brodnitz, "The Most In-Demand Skills for 2024," *LinkedIn Talent* (blog), February 8, 2024, https://www.linkedin.com/business/talent/blog/talent-strategy/linkedin-most-in-demand-hard-and-soft-skills.

3. Tara Swart, *The Source: The Secrets of the Universe, the Science of the Brain* (HarperOne, 2019).

4. Elizabeth A. Kensinger, "Remembering the Details: Effects of Emotion," *Memory and Cognition* 37, no. 8 (2009): 1165–1177.

CHAPTER 9

1. Michael Hughes, "Leadership from a Dancing Guy," YouTube, June 12, 2010, https://www.youtube.com/watch?v=hO8MwBZl-Vc.

2. Edward Deci and Richard Ryan, *Intrinsic Motivation and Self-Determination in Human Behavior* (Springer Science and Business Media, 1985).

3. Ryan Pendell, "Employee Engagement Strategies: Fixing the World's $8.8 Trillion Workplace Problem," *Gallup Workplace*, September 11, 2023, https://www.gallup.com/workplace/393497/world-trillion-workplace-problem.aspx.

4. Marian C. Diamond, David Krech, and Mark R. Rosenzweig, "The Effects of an Enriched Environment on the Histology of the Rat Cerebral Cortex," *Journal of Comparative Neurology* 123, no. 1 (1964): 111–120.

CHAPTER 10

1. G. R. Stephenson, "Cultural Acquisition of a Specific Learned Response Among Rhesus Monkeys, Macaca Mulattaj," *First Congress of the International Primatological Society* (1967): 280–288, https://www.scribd.com/doc/106891948/ Stephenson-G-R-1967-Cultural-Acquisition-of-a-Specific-Learned-Response -Among-Rhesus-Monkeys-in-Starek-D-Schneider-R-And-Kuhn-H-J-Eds.

2. Korn Ferry, "Redefining a Skills-Based Organization," November 12, 2023, https://www.kornferry.com/insights/featured-topics/organizational -transformation/redefining-a-skills-based-organization.

CHAPTER 11

1. Illustrations and resources can be found at www.leadershipanatomyinmotion.com.

2. Q. Hamirani, "Decisiveness Is the Crucible of Effective Leadership," *Forbes*, August 23, 2024, https://www.forbes.com/sites/qhamirani/2024/08/23/ decisiveness-is-the-crucible-of-effective-leadership.

3. Sheetal Pansare, "Predictive Analytics in Global Trade: Forecasting Market Trends with AI," *Global Trade*, June 20, 2024, https://www.globaltrademag.com/ predictive-analytics-in-global-trade-forecasting-market-trends-with-ai/.

4. R. J. Messineo, "What Is a KPI Report, and How Do I Create One?" *ClearPoint Strategy*, accessed June 11, 2025, https://www.clearpointstrategy.com/blog/ what-is-a-kpi-report-how-do-i-create-one.

CHAPTER 12

1. Erica Ariel Fox, *Winning from Within: A Breakthrough Method for Leading, Living, and Lasting Change* (Harper Business, 2013).

2. Kim B. Clark, Jonathan R. Clark, and Erin E. Clark, *Leading Through: Activating the Soul, Heart, and Mind of Leadership* (Harvard Business Review Press, 2024).

3. C. Otto Scharmer, *Theory U: Leading from the Future as It Emerges* (Society for Organizational Learning, 2007).

4. Illustrations and resources can be found at www.leadershipanatomyinmotion.com.

5. Norman Doidge, *The Brain That Changes Itself: Stories of Personal Triumph from the Frontiers of Brain Science* (Penguin Books, 2007).

6. Katherine Woollett and Eleanor A. Maguire, "Acquiring 'the Knowledge' of London's Layout Drives Structural Brain Changes," *Current Biology* 21, no. 24 (2011): 2109–2114.

7. Carl Jung, *Aion: Researches into the Phenomenology of the Self*, trans. R. F. C. Hull (Princeton University Press, 1951), 8.

8. Albert Mehrabian, *Silent Messages* (Wadsworth, 1971).

9. Judee K. Burgoon, Laura K. Guerrero, and Kory Floyd, *Nonverbal Communication*, 7th ed. (Routledge, 2016).

10. Tara Swart, *The Source: The Secrets of the Universe, the Science of the Brain* (HarperOne, 2019).

11. Jürgen Beckmann and Michael Kellmann, *Sport, Recovery, and Performance: Interdisciplinary Insights* (Routledge, 2017).

12. Britta K. Hölzel, James Carmody, Mark Vangel, et al., "Mindfulness Practice Leads to Increases in Regional Brain Gray Matter Density," *NeuroImage* 19, no. 1 (2011): 36–42.

13. Daniel Goleman and Richard Boyatzis, "Social Intelligence and the Biology of Leadership," *Harvard Business Review* 86, no. 9 (2008): 74–81.

14. Marc G. Berman, John Jonides, and Stephen Kaplan, "The Cognitive Benefits of Interacting with Nature," *Psychological Science* 19, no. 12 (2008): 1207–1212.

15. Sian L. Beilock, *How the Body Knows Its Mind: The Surprising Power of the Physical Environment to Influence How You Think and Feel* (Atria Books, 2015).

CHAPTER 13

1. Shwetha Nair, Mark Sagar, John Sollers, Nathan Consedine, and Elizabeth Broadbent, "Do Slumped and Upright Postures Affect Stress Responses? A Randomized Trial," *Health Psychology* 34, no. 6 (2015): 632–641.

2. Sian L. Beilock, *Choke: What Secrets of the Brain Reveal About Getting It Right When You Have To* (Atria, 2011).

3. Dirk Devos, Manon de Wit, and Robert Lubberding, *Leading from Behind: Turn Anxiety into Courage* (LID, 2018).

4. Illustrations and resources can be found at www.leadershipanatomyinmotion.com.

5. Jordi Quoidbach, Daniel T. Gilbert, and Timothy D. Wilson, "The End of History Illusion," *Science* 339, no. 6115 (2013): 96–98.

CHAPTER 14

1. Elaine Hatfield, John T. Cacioppo, and Richard L. Rapson, *Emotional Contagion* (Cambridge University Press, 1994).

2.   Sigal G. Barsade and Donald E. Gibson, "Why Does Affect Matter in Organizations?" *Academy of Management Perspectives* 21, no. 1 (2007): 36–59.

3.   Kevin Laczkowski, Tao Tan, and Matthias Winter, "The Numbers Behind Successful Transformations," McKinsey & Company, October 17, 2019, https://www.mckinsey.com/capabilities/transformation/our-insights/the-numbers-behind-successful-transformations.

4.   John P. Kotter, *Leading Change* (Harvard Business School Press, 1996); Michael Beer and Nitin Nohria, "Cracking the Code of Change," *Harvard Business Review* 78, no. 3 (May–June 2000): 133–141.

INDEX

ABOUT THE AUTHOR

LOUISA LORAN is a global executive advisor and board member with more than two decades of leadership experience at Diageo, Maersk, and Google—companies that all outpaced their industries during her tenure.

She brings cross-industry expertise and a strong track record of leading profitable transformations from within—building billion-dollar businesses, repositioning global brands, and navigating executive teams through complex shifts. Known for connecting analytical and human insights, Louisa draws on deep operational experience and strategically uses technology, data, and AI to drive sustainable results.

She also serves on the board of a private equity firm and a globally leading business school. A lifelong learner, Louisa has deepened her perspective through advanced studies at Stanford, IMD, and INSEAD and neuroscience studies at MIT. She also expands her perspective daily through interactions with people navigating change, turning those insights into apt situational guidance for the businesses and leaders she advises.